Shakespeare, The Cavalier Poets,

Milton & Others

Charles Norrington

The Pentland Press Limited
Edinburgh • Cambridge • Durham

First published in 1994 by
The Pentland Press Ltd.
1 Hutton Close
South Church
Bishop Auckland
Durham

ISBN 1 85821 079 8

Typeset by CBS, Felixstowe, Suffolk
Printed and bound by Antony Rowe Ltd., Chippenham

Foreword

Many schools and friends in the U.K. and Australia have already received parts of this collection in typescript. However, requests have been made for a more permanent record.

I, therefore, offer this book of quotations to put the compendium 'under one roof', hoping that it kindles enthusiasm among the young and serves as an 'aide-mémoire' for the 'cognoscenti'.

I have to thank many friends, old and new, who have encouraged me, including teachers who have kindly made suggestions and contributions.

I am most grateful to my niece Catherine for typing scripts, to my wife for her continual patience and support and, above all, to Margery and Betty Beavis.

Charles Norrington

Member of 'The Queen's English Society'

Preface

Shakespeare, The Bible,

Milton & Others

Part I

Shakespeare

– In Daily Conversation

SHAKESPEARE IN OUR DAILY CONVERSATION

This anthology is not primarily concerned with Shakespeare's well-known quotations; rather it is to record his words and expressions which are so apt that we still use them today.

When reading the bard's 37 plays his greatness was borne upon me anew: his humanity; his marvellous choice of words; and his patriotism which shines like a silver thread among the gold in his Histories.

Appropriately, William Shakespeare was born on St. George's Day on 23rd of April, 1564 and he died fifty-two years later – also on St. George's Day.

THE TWO GENTLEMEN OF VERONA

To make a virtue of necessity	IV, 1

THE TAMING OF THE SHREW

You're *a baggage*	Intro. 1
I'll *not budge* an inch	Intro. 1
. . . a goodly nap	Intro. 1
I found the effect of *love in idleness*	Intro. 1
. . . to comb your *noddle* with a three-legg'd stool	I, i
And if you *break the ice* and do this feat	I, ii
. . . or an old trot with *ne'er a tooth in her head*	
An *eyesore* to our solemn festival	III, 2
You may be *jogging* whiles your boots are green	III, 2
. . . To thy cold comfort	IV, 1
. . . and thereby hangs a tale	IV, 1
This is the way to *kill a wife with kindness*	IV, 1
'Tis *10 to 1* it maimed you two outright	V, 2
The more fool you . . .	V, 2
. . . bandy word for word	V, 2
. . . 'Tis a wonder	V, 2

A COMEDY OF ERRORS

There's no rhyme or reason	II, 2
'Tis high time that I were hence	III, 2
There is something in the wind	III, 1
We must have a long spoon that must eat with the Devil (Also Chaucer)	IV, 3

LOVE'S LABOUR LOST

. . . in May's new fangled shows (Also Chaucer)	I, 1
That were fast and loose . . .	II, 1
I'll prove her fair, or *talk* till *doomsday* here	IV, 3
. . . some slight *zany*	V, 2
. . . played foul play	V, 2

A MIDSUMMER NIGHT'S DREAM

Single blessedness	I, 1
The course of true love never did run smooth	II, 2

THE MERCHANT OF VENICE

The Devil can cite scripture to his purpose	I, 3
With bated breath	I, 3
It is a wise father that knows his own child	II, 1
But, at length, *truth will out*	II, 1
Thou art my own *flesh and blood*	II, 1
The *short and long* of it is . . .	II, 1
. . . I have ne'er a tongue in my head	II, 1
The portrait of *a blinking idiot*	II, 9
Presenting me a *schedule*	II, 9
. . . green-eyed jealousy	III, 2
The pound of flesh	IV, 1
We should day with the *Antipodes* if you would walk in the absence of the sun	V, 1

THE MERRY WIVES OF WINDSOR

. . . than the 100th Psalm to the tune "*Greensleeves*"	II, 1
The world's mine oyster	II, 2

This is the *long and short* of it	II, 2
Let us not be laughing stocks	III, 1
I cannot tell what *the dickens* his name is	III, 2
A cannon will shoot *point-blank*	III, 2
As good luck would have it	III, 5
A man of my kidney	III, 5

MUCH ADO ABOUT NOTHING

O, Lord!	I, 1
. . . a heart sound as a bell	III, 2
Are you good men and true?	III, 3
Will you not eat your words?	IV, 1
. . . flesh and blood	V, 1
Some of us would *lie low*	V,

AS YOU LIKE IT

. . . and there they live like the old *Robin Hood* of England	I, 1
Sweet are the uses of adversity	II, 1
They are often tarred over with the surgery of our *sheep* (not *ship*)	
I will follow thee to *the last gasp*	II, 3
The more fool I . . .	II, 4
Welcome, . . . *fall to*	II, 7
Well said, that was *laid on with a trowel*	II, 7
Thou art in a *parlous state*	III, 2
With bag and baggage	III, 2
. . . and *conned* them out of rings	III, 2
His leg is but *so-so*	III, 5
Can one have too much of a good thing?	IV, 1
More *new fangled* than an ape	IV, 1
'Tis *meat and drink* to me	V, 1

TWELFTH NIGHT

TROILUS AND CRESSIDA

MEASURE FOR MEASURE

ALL'S WELL THAT ENDS WELL

PERICLES, PRINCE OF TYRE

THE WINTER'S TALE

... or else 'twere *hard luck*   V, 2

CYMBELINE

His name is *last gasp*	I, 5
I have lost today at *bowls*	II, 1
The game is up	III, 3
... in hugger-mugger to inter him	III, 3
The gates of monarchs are arc'd so high that giants may *jet* through	III, 3
I have not slept one wink	III, 4
... and put my clouted *brogues* from off my feet	IV, 2

THE TEMPEST

O, my heart bleeds!	I, 2
Where the devil did he learn our language?	II, 2
Keep a good tongue in thy head	III, 2
Caliban: ... there thou mayst *brain* him	III, 2
... shall *hoodwink* all mischance	IV, 1
... are melted into air, *into thin air*	IV, 1
I am struck to the quick	V, 1
O, brave new world!	V, 1
How camest thou in *this pickle*?	V, 1

TITUS ANDRONICUS

... the *post* is come, have you any *letters* ...	
The hunt is up	II, 2
... our withers are unwrung	III, 2
Ay, that's my boy!	IV, 1
How all occasions do inform against me	IV, 2

ROMEO AND JULIET

The weakest goes to the wall	I, 1
Tis a pity you lived *at odds* so long	I, 2
Ladies that have their *toes unplagued by corns*	I, 5
Parting is such sweet sorrow	II, 2
What's in a name? That which we call the rose by any other name would smell as sweet	II, 2
Thy wits run the *wild-goose chase*	II, 4
If you lead her into *a fool's paradise*	II, 4
We will make *short work*	II, 5
A plague on both your houses	III, 1
Where have you been *gadding*?	III, 2

JULIUS CAESAR

It was Greek to me	I, 3
... that is no *fleoring tell-tale*	I, 3
I never stood on ceremony	II, 2
The multitude, *beside themselves* with fear	III, 1
... to have an *itching palm*	III, 3

HAMLET, PRINCE OF DENMARK

In my mind's eye	I, 2
A countenance more in sorrow than in anger	I, 2
... to the manner born	II, 4
Though this be madness there is method in it	II, 2
'twas caviare to the general (i.e. the public)	II, 2
Still *harping* on my daughter	II, 2
'The Mousetrap' - title of play within play	II, 2
... natural shocks that *flesh is heir to*	III, 1
... the law's delay	III, 1
When we have *shuffled off this mortal coil*	III, 1
Suit the action to the word	III, 2

. . . to the top of my bent	III, 2
It out-herods Herod	III, 2
A King of *shreds and patches*	III, 4
I must be cruel to be kind	III, 4
Hoist with his own petard²	III, 4
When sorrows come - they come in battalions	IV, 5
. . . in *hugger-mugger*	IV, 5
A ministering angel	V, 1
It did me *yeoman's service*	V, 2
. . . into a towering passion	V, 2
. . . more germane to the matter	V, 2
Popp'd in between my election and my hopes	V, 2

OTHELLO

I will *wear* my *heart upon my sleeve*	I, 1
Have you lost your wits,	I, 1
To suckle fools and chronicle *small beer*	II, 1
Thy honesty and love doth mince the matter	II, 3
Jealousy - the green-eyed monster	III, 3
Pride, pomp and circumstance	III, 3
. . . a foregone conclusion	III, 3
'Tis neither here nor there	IV, 3
And have their palates both for *sweet and sour*	IV, 3
. . . it makes us or mars us	V, 1
One that loved not wisely but too well	V, 2
Here is my journey's end	V, 2

TIMON OF ATHENS

I feel it *upon my bones*	III, 6
We have seen better days	IV, 2
It is but *botched*	IV, 3

KING LEAR

I will hold my tongue	I, 4
Nor tripped neither, ye base *football* player	I, 4
Thy wit will ne'er go *slipshod*	I, 5
. . . a man more sinned against than sinning	III, 2
This is the foul fiend *flibberty-gibbet*	III, 4
Ay, every inch a King	IV, 6
The wheel has come full circle	V, 3

MACBETH

. . . too full of the *milk of human kindness*	I, 5
Let us *shift away*	II, 3
. . . to the *crack of doom*	IV, 1
. . . in one fell swoop	IV, 3
At least we'll die with harness on our back	V, 5
I bear a charmed life	V, 6
. . . Full of sound and fury	V, 5

ANTONY AND CLEOPATRA

My salad days, when I was green in judgement	I, 5
. . . her infinite variety	II, 2
Lets to billiards	II, 3
He should not have nicked his captainship	III, 13
Like a right gipsy hath at fast and loose beguiled me	IV, 12

CORIOLANUS

They have had *an inkling* . . . what we intend to do	I, 2
Made you *against the grain* to voice him consul?	II, 3

Alone I did it	V, 6
Let's make the best of it	V, 6

KING HENRY VI (Part 1)

They are *hare-brained* slaves	I, 2
I will not *budge* a foot	I, 3
Thou wolf in sheep's array	I, 3
See the *coast's cleared*	I, 3
Quid for Quo	V, 3
Burn her! *Hanging is too good*	V, 4

KING HENRY VI (Part 2)

Rule the roast (Also Chaucer)	I, 1
Why does he *knit his brows?*	I, 2
I would remove these tedious *stumbling blocks*	I, 2
His *far-fet* policy	III, 1
Smooth runs the water where the brook runs deep	III, 1
Thrice armed is he that hath his quarrel just	III, 2
As dead as a door-nail	IV, 10

KING HENRY VI (Part 3)

Be that as it may . . .	I, 1
To make *a shambles* of the Parliament House	I, 1
Post-haste	II, 1
Ill blows the wind that profits nobody	II, 1
The smallest worm will turn being trodden on	II, 2
The *bloody minded* Queen (Also Chaucer)	II, 6
I cannot brook delay	III, 2
Tis better said than done	III, 2
. . . both *are birds of self same feather*	III, 3
By fair means or foul	IV, 2

Strike now, or else the iron cools	V, 1
I need not add fuel to your fire	V, 4

RICHARD III

The winter of our discontent	I, 1
I myself in *grace and favour*	III, 4
Dispatch, my lord, *make a short shrift*	III, 4
The citizens are mum and speak no word	III, 7
Welcome, my lord, *I dance attendance* here	III, 7
The King's name is a *tower of strength*	V, 3
Stir *with the lark* tomorrow	V, 3
Let's to it *pell-mell*	V, 3

RICHARD II

Lions make leopards tame, but not *change their spots*	I, 1
There's no virtue like necessity (Also Chaucer)	II, 2
. . . everything *at six and seven*	II, 2
. . . Tut, tut!	II, 3
. . . befeared and *kill with looks*	III, 2
God save the King!	IV, 1
For God's sake!	V, 3
Yet I'll *hammer it out*	V, 3
. . . like silly beggars	V, 5
Since pride must have its fall	V, 6
My lord, will't please you *to fall to*	V, 6

KING JOHN

Look where *3/4d* goes . . .	I, 1
Your face hath got *£500* a year	I, 1
You sell your face for *5d* and 'tis dear	I, 1

. . . fiery kindred spirits!	II, 1
Zounds! I never was so b'thumped with words	II, 1
since I first call'd my brother's father *Dad*	
Sticking together in calamity	III, 4
I will sit *quiet as a lamb*	IV, 1
I would be *as merry as the day is long*	IV, 1
It is apparent *foul play*	IV, 2
To *paint* the lily	IV, 2
. . . but now I breathe again	IV, 2
I do not ask you much . . . I beg *cold comfort*	V, 7

KING HENRY IV (Part 1)

He made me *mad* to see him shine	I, 1
. . . scoured to nothing with *perpetual motion*	I, 2
Give the devil his due	I, 2
When time is ripe	I, 3
. . . I'll be hanged	II, 2
God knows what	II, 2
. . . the *stony-hearted* villains	II, 2
. . . I could brain him	II, 2
Show it *a fair pair of heels*	II, 3
. . . not an inch further	II, 4
. . . 8 shillings and 6 pence	II, 4
. . . the more the pity	II, 4
. . . and I'll *send him packing*	II, 4
Tell truth and shame the devil	III, 1
That would set my *teeth on edge*	III, 1
As true as I live	III, 1
A good *mouth filling* oath	III, 1
We shall o'erturn it *topsy-turvy*	IV, 1
I'll not march with them, *that's flat*	IV, 2
The news of hurlyburly innovation	V, 1
. . . such *water-colours* to impaint his cause	V, 1
A hair-brain'd Hotspur	V, 2
The better part of valour is discretion	V, 4

KING HENRY IV (Part 2)

I have been *fubbed off, fubbed off, fubbed off*	II, 1
He hath *eaten me out of house and home* (Also Chaucer)	II, 1
What the devil hast thou brought here?	II, 4
Thy wish was father, Harry, to that thought	IV, 1
Not the ill-wind which blows no man good	V, 3
And *helter-skelter* have I rode	V, 3

KING HENRY V

Playing the mouse in the absence of the cat	I, 2
Even at the turning of the tide	II, 3
. . . and said they were *devils incarnate*	II, 3
The King's heart of gold	IV, 1
The empty vessel maketh the most sound	IV, 4

KING HENRY VIII

For goodness sake!	Prologue
No *pie is freed from* his ambitious *finger*	I, 1
When the way is made and *paved with gold*	I, 1
I would not be a queen *for all the world*	II, 3
. . . to be perk'd up	II, 3
Do you look for *ale and cakes* here?	V, 4
The *High and Mighty* Princess Elizabeth	V, 5

Part II

The Bible

– In daily conversation

THE BIBLE IN OUR DAILY CONVERSATION

This collection of words and expressions from the authorised (King James I) version of the Holy Bible is intended to show how many we still use in our daily parlance. Many have been varied or shortened in course of time, but the poetry of the Elizabethan translators shines through. Most of them are so apt that they remain unaltered.

A similar distillation from the plays of Shakespeare reveals several items also in the Bible. He would have been writing them during the period when other leading men of letters were at work on the Bible. Perhaps they borrowed from each other and all shared in England's golden age of literature.

And God *saw the light*	Genesis	Ch.1	v.4
Am I my brother's keeper?	Genesis	Ch.4	v.9
Esau selleth his birthright for a *mess of pottage*	Genesis	Ch.25	v.34
. . . there was *corn in Egypt*	Genesis	Ch.42	v.1
Ye shall *eat the fat of the land*	Genesis	Ch.45	v.18
. . . See that ye fall not by the way	Genesis	Ch.45	v.24
A land flowing with milk and honey	Exodus	Ch.3	v.8
Ye shall no more give the people *straw to make brick*	Exodus	Ch.5	v.7
Even darkness which may be felt	Exodus	Ch.10	v.21
In the land of Egypt, when we sat by the *fleshpots*	Exodus	Ch.16	v.3
. . . it is *Manna* (from heaven)	Exodus	Ch.16	v.15
. . . eye for eye - tooth for tooth	Exodus	Ch.21	v.24
Thou art a *stiff-necked* people	Exodus	Ch.33	v.3
. . . the *scapegoat* . . . to make an atonement	Levit.	Ch,16	v.10
. . . nor put a stumbling-block before the blind	Levit.	Ch.19	v.11
Thou shalt not *bear any grudg*e against thy people	Levit.	Ch.19	v.18
. . . and ye shall eat it until it come out at your nostrils	Numbers	Ch.11	v.20
. . . the man which Moses sent *to spy out the land*	Numbers	Ch.13	v.16
. . . ye shall know my *breach of promise*	Numbers	Ch.14	v.34
. . . we will go by the *king's highway*	Numbers	Ch.20	v.17
. . . be sure your sin will find you out	Numbers	Ch.32	v.23
. . . that *taketh his name in vain*	Deut.	Ch.5	v.11
. . . and *with all thy might*	Deut.	Ch.6	v.5
. . . the Lord *rooted them out*	Deut.	Ch.29	v.28
He kept him as *the apple of his eye*	Deut.	Ch.32	v.10
. . . until all the people were passed *clean over* Jordan	Joshua	Ch.3	v.17
. . . they shall be as *thorns in your sides*	Judges	Ch.2	v.3
The stars in their courses fought against Sisera	Judges	Ch.5	v.20
He and 300 men were *faint yet pursuing* them	Judges	Ch.8	v.4
. . . and he smote them hip and thigh . . .	Judges	Ch.15	v.8
The people arose *as one man*	Judges	Ch.20	v.8
. . . sling stones at *an hair breadth* and not miss	Judges	Ch.20	v.16
A man after his own heart	I Sam.	Ch.3	v.14
Samuel judged Israel . . . and went from year to year in circuit	I Sam.	Ch.7	v.16
Samuel heard all the words of the people			

and *rehearsed* them to the Lord	I Sam.	Ch.8	v.21
. . . the ears of everyone . . . shall tingle . . .	I Sam.	Ch.3	v.11
God save the King	I Sam.	Ch.10	v.24
Jonathan gave his *artillery* unto his lad	I Sam.	Ch.20	v.40
. . . and *scrabbled* upon the doors of the gate	I Sam.	Ch.21	v.13
"Behold! I have *played the fool*"	I Sam.	Ch.26	v.21
Thy blood upon thy head	II Sam.	Ch.1	v.16
How are the mighty fallen!	II Sam.	Ch.1	v.19
. . . and make me a *couple* of cakes	II Sam.	Ch.13	v.6
By my God have I *leaped over a wall*	II Sam.	Ch.22	v.30
. . . and a certain man *drew a bow at a venture*	I Kings	Ch.22	v.34
. . . set thine house in order	II Kings	Ch.20	v.1
. . . *over and above* all that I have prepared . . .	I Chron.	Ch.29	v.3
. . . there is no *respect of persons* with the Lord our God	II Chron.	Ch.6	v.3
. . . with all his heart	II Chron.	Ch.34	v.31
. . . but he . . . *hardened his heart*	II Chron.	Ch.36	v.13
. . . the people gathered themselves together *as one man*	Ezra	Ch.3	v.1
. . . she obtained *grace and favour* in the king's sight	Esther	Ch.2	v.17
. . . and many lay in *sackcloth with ashes*	Esther	Ch.4	v.3
. . . If *I hold my tongue*, I shall *give up the ghost*	Job	Ch.13	v.19
I am escaped *with the skin of my teeth*	Job	Ch.19	v.20
Seeing *the root of the matter* is found in me	Job	Ch.19	v.28
Out of the mouths of babes and sucklings	Psalms (also Matt.)	Ch.8 Ch.21	v.2 v.16
Let not man have *the upper hand*	Psalms	Ch.9	v.9
Thou hast given him his *heart's desire*	Psalms	Ch.21	v.2
All they that see me *laugh me to scorn*	Psalms	Ch.22	v.7
. . . in the land of the living . . .	Psalms	Ch.27	v.15
. . . my cup runneth over . . .	Psalms	Ch.23	v.5
Remember, O Lord, thy *tender mercies* and *loving kindness*	Psalms	Ch.25	v.6
. . . the poor and the needy . . .	Psalms	Ch.35	v.10
Deep calleth to deep	Psalms	Ch.42	v.7
. . . all the ends of the earth	Psalms	Ch.65	v.5

. . . and she that tarried at home *divided the spoil*	Psalms	Ch.68 v.12
Renew a *right spirit* within me	Psalms	Ch.51 v.10
His enemies shall *lick the dust*	Psalms	Ch.72 v.9
They go from *strength to strength*	Psalms	Ch.84 v.7
Our years are *three score and ten*	Psalms	Ch.90 v.10
. . . are *at their wit's end*	Psalms	Ch.107v.27
This is the Lord's doing	Psalms	Ch.118v.23
Put not your trust in princes	Psalms	Ch.146v.3
Surely the net is spread in vain in the sight of any bird	Proverbs	Ch.1 v.17
Sharp as a *two-edged sword*	Proverbs	Ch.5 v.4
Hope deferred maketh the heart sick	Proverbs	Ch.13 v.12
He that *spareth the rod* hateth his son	Proverbs	Ch.13 v.24
A soft answer turneth away wrath	Proverbs	Ch.15 v.1
A word spoken in due season	Proverbs	Ch.15 v.23
Look not upon the wine when it is red	Proverbs	Ch.23 v.31
Heap *coals of fire* upon is head	Proverbs	Ch.25 v.22
The righteous are *as bold as a lion*	Proverbs	Ch.28 v.1
There is no new thing under the sun	Eccles.	Ch.1 v.8
Dead flies cause the ointment to send forth a stinking savour	Eccles.	Ch.10 v.1
Cast thy bread upon the waters	Eccles.	Ch.11 v.1
Their name liveth for evermore	Eccles.	Ch.44 v.14
They shall beat swords into plowshares	Isaiah	Ch.2 v.4
. . . and grind the faces of the poor	Isaiah	Ch.3 v.15
Let us eat and drink; for tomorrow we shall die	Isaiah	Ch.22 v.13
	also I Cor.	Ch.15 v.32
. . . and for *durable clothing*	Isaiah	Ch.23 v.18
The desert shall rejoice and *blossom as the rose*	Isaiah	Ch.35 v.1
Lo, thou trustest in the staff of *this broken reed*	Isaiah	Ch.36 v.3
The voice of him that *crieth in the wilderness*	Isaiah	Ch.40 v.3
The nations are as a *drop in a bucket*	Isaiah	Ch.40 v.15
There is *no peace*, saith the Lord, *unto the wicked*	Isaiah	Ch.48 v.22
. . . I have *laboured in vain*	Isaiah	Ch.49 v.4
. . . to speak a *word in season*	Isaiah	Ch.50 v.4
They shall see *eye to eye*	Isaiah	Ch.52 v.8
. . . he is brought *as a lamb to the slaughter*	Isaiah	Ch.53 v.7

. . . the land of the living	Isaiah	Ch.53 v.3
. . . take up the *stumbling-block* out of the way	Isaiah	Ch.57 v.14
Set thine house in order	Isaiah	Ch.58 v.1
. . . holier than thou	Isaiah	Ch.65 v.5
Arise, shine; for thy light is come	Isaiah	Ch.60 v.1
Why *gaddest thou about* so much?	Jeremiah	Ch.2 v.36
Can the Ethiopian change his skin, or the *leopard his spots*?	Jeremiah	Ch.13 v.23
. . . smote Jeremiah and put him in the stocks	Jeremiah	Ch.20 v.2
Cursed be the day wherein I was born	Jeremiah	Ch.20 v.14
His teeth shall be *set on edge*	Jeremiah	Ch.31 v.30
He cut it with *the penknife*	Jeremiah	Ch.36 v.23
Lament, and run *to and fro* by the hedges	Jeremiah	Ch.49 v.3
There was a continual *diet* given him	Jeremiah	Ch.52 v.34
They *hiss* and *gnash* the teeth	Lamentations	Ch.2 v.16
. . . and all knees shall be *weak as water*	Ezekiel	Ch.7 v.17
. . . as if a *wheel* had been in the midst of a *wheel*	Ezekiel	Ch.10 v.10
The fathers have eaten *sour grapes*	Ezekiel	Ch.18 v.2
The King of Babylon *stood at the parting of the way*	Ezekiel	Ch.21 v.21
I will take the *stony heart* out of their flesh	Ezekiel	Ch.11 v.19
. . . that Israel go no more *astray* from me	Ezekiel	Ch.14 v.11
. . . for fuel to the fire	Ezekiel	Ch.21 v.32
. . . his blood shall be upon his own head	Ezekiel	Ch.18 v.2
. . . his feet . . . of clay	Daniel	Ch.2 v.52
. . . a man's hand . . . *wrote upon* the plaister *of the wall*	Daniel	Ch.5 v.5
Thou art weighed in the balance and found wanting	Daniel	Ch.5 v.27
According to the law of the Medes and Persians	Daniel	Ch.6 v.8
. . . and cast him into a *den of lions*	Daniel	Ch.6 v.16
. . . whose garment was white as snow	Daniel	Ch.7 v.9
. . . the years that the locust hath eaten	Joel	Ch.2 v.25
Hold thy tongue	Amos	Ch.6 v.1
They shall beat . . . their spears into *pruning hooks*	Micah	Ch.4 v.3
. . . and ye have snuffed at it	Malachi	Ch.1 v.13
Man shall not live by bread alone	St. Matt.	Ch.4 v.4
Ye are *the salt of the earth*	St. Matt.	Ch.5 v.13
It is thenceforth *good for nothing*	St. Matt.	Ch.5 v.13

. . . an eye for an eye	St. Matt.	Ch.5	v.38
. . . there shall be weeping and gnashing of teeth	St. Matt.	Ch.8	v.2
Neither do men *light a candle* and *put it under a bushel*	St. Matt.	Ch.5	v.15
Let not thy left hand know what thy right hand doeth	St. Matt.	Ch.6	v.3
No man can serve two masters	St. Matt.	Ch.6	v.24
Ye cannot serve God and mammon	St. Matt.	Ch.6	v.24
Many are called, but few are chosen	St. Matt.	Ch.22	v.14
. . . as a shepherd divideth his sheep from the goats	St. Matt	Ch.25	v.32
The spirit indeed is willing but the flesh is weak	St. Matt.	Ch.26	v.41
Well done, thou good and faithful servant	St. Matt.	Ch.25	v.21
Sufficient unto the day is the evil thereof	St. Matt.	Ch.6	v.34
Why considereth thou *the mote* that is *in thy brother's eye*, but considereth not *the beam that is in thine own eye*?	St. Matt.	Ch.7	v.3
Neither cast ye your pearls before swine	St. Matt.	Ch.7	v.6
Beware of false prophets which come to you *in sheep's clothing* but inwardly they are *ravening wolves*	St. Matt.	Ch.7	v.15
Neither do men put *new wine in old bottles*	St. Matt.	Ch.9	v.17
He that is not with me is against me	St. Matt.	Ch.12	v.30
	(also Luke)	Ch.11	v.23
Some seeds *fell by the wayside*	St. Matt.	Ch.13	v.4
. . . the crumbs which fall from the rich man's table	St. Matt.	Ch.15	v.27
Can ye discern the *signs of the times*?	St. Matt.	Ch.16	v.3
Get thee behind me Satan	St. Matt.	Ch.16	v.23
. . . better that a *millstone were hanged about his neck*	St. Matt.	Ch.18	v.6
Many that are first shall be last; and the last shall be first	St. Matt.	Ch.19	v.30
	(also Mark)	Ch.10	v.31
. . . borne the burden and heat of the day	St. Matt.	Ch.20	v.12
. . . ye have made it a *den of thieves*	St. Matt.	Ch.21	v.13
Pilate . . . took water and *washed his hands*	St. Matt.	Ch.27	v.24
Simon of Cyrene; him they compelled *to bear the cross*	St. Matt.	Ch.27	v.32

Part II

. . . and some fell upon stony ground	St. Mark	Ch.4	v.5
My name is legion; for we are many	St. Mark	Ch.5	v.9
. . . clothed, and in his right mind	St. Mark	Ch.5	v.15
For he that hath, to him shall be given, and he that hath not from him shall be taken even that which he hath	St. Mark	Ch.4	v.25
For ye have the poor with you always	St. Mark	Ch.14	v.7
Shake off the dust under your feet	St. Mark	Ch.6	v.11
. . . The voice of one crying in the wilderness	St. Luke	Ch.3	v.4
They don't practise what they preach	St. Luke	Ch.3	v.4
Unto him that smiteth thee on one cheek offer also the other	St. Luke	Ch.6	v.29
Physician, heal thyself	St. Luke	Ch.4	v.23
The Labourer is worthy of his hire (Also Chaucer)	St. Luke	Ch.10	v.7
A certain (good) Samaritan . . . had compassion etc.	St. Luke	Ch.10	v.33
Seek and ye shall find	St. Luke	Ch.11	v.9
. . . shall be proclaimed from the housetops	St. Luke	Ch.12	v.3
Eat, drink and be merry	St. Luke	Ch.12	v.19
Go out into the *byways and hedges*	St. Luke	Ch.14	v.23
There wasted his substance with *riotous living*	St. Luke	Ch.15	v.13
Bring hither the *fatted calf,* and *kill it*	St. Luke	Ch.15	v.23
Give an account of thy stewardship	St. Luke	Ch.16	v.2
It rained fire and brimstone	St. Luke	Ch.17	v.29
A prophet hath no honour in his own country	St. John	Ch.4	v.44
He that is without sin, let him cast the stone	St. John	Ch.8	v.7
Your Lord and Master	St. John	Ch.13	v.14
. . . to whom I shall *give the sop*	St. John	Ch.13	v.26
. . . doubting Thomas etc.	St. John	Ch.21	v.27
It is hard for thee *to kick against the pricks*	Acts	Ch.9	v.5
God is no respecter of persons	Acts	Ch.10	v.34
. . . and there *fell from his eyes* as it had been *scales*	Acts	Ch.9	v.18
. . . a man after mine own heart	Acts	Ch.10	v.22
They have turned the world upside down	Acts	Ch.12	v.6
. . . a citizen of no mean city	Acts	Ch.21	v.39
Paul, thou art *beside yourself*	Acts	Ch.26	v.24
The Gentiles . . . are a law unto themselves	Romans	Ch.2	v.14
God forbid	Romans	Ch.3	v.6

The wages of sin is death	Romans	Ch.6	v.23
. . . because *short work* will the Lord *make* upon earth	Romans	Ch.9	v.28
Thou shalt *heap coals of fire upon his head*	Romans	Ch.12	v.20
I am made *all things to all men*	I Corin.	Ch.9	v.22
. . . Our fathers were *under the cloud*	I Corin.	Ch.10	v.1
Whatsoever is sold *in the shambles*, that eat	I Corin.	Ch.10	v.25
As one born out of due time	I Corin.	Ch.15	v.8
In a moment, *in the twinkling of an eye*; at *the last trump*	I Corin.	Ch.15	v.52
God loveth a cheerful giver	II Corin.	Ch.9	v.7
Ye suffer fools gladly	II Corin.	Ch.11	v.19
There was given to me a *thorn in the flesh*	II Corin.	Ch.12	v.7
I rather glory in my infirmities	II Corin.	Ch.12	v.9
I conferred not with flesh and blood	Galatians	Ch.1	v.16
Ye are fallen from grace	Galatians	Ch.5	v.4
Every man shall *bear his own burden*	Galatians	Ch.6	v.5
. . . whose God is their belly	Philip.	Ch.3	v.19
(Also Chaucer)			
. . . with *fear and trembling*	Philip.	Ch.2	v.12
It is a shame even to speak	Ephesians	Ch.5	v.12
I am with you in spirit	Coloss.	Ch.2	v.5
Let your speech be alway with grace, *seasoned with salt*	Coloss.	Ch.4	v.6
. . . and labour of love	I Thess.	Ch.1	v.3
What manner of men?	I Thess.	Ch.1	v.5
. . . coming as a thief in the night	I. Thess.	Ch.5	v.2
. . . if any man would not work, neither would he eat	II Thess.	Ch.3	v.10
Not greedy of *filthy lucre*	I Tim.	Ch.3	v.3
. . . but refuse profane and *old wives'* fables	I Tim.	Ch.4	v.7
Use a little wine for thy stomach's sake	I Tim.	Ch.5	v.23
The love of money is the root of all evil	I Tim.	Ch.6	v.10
(Also Chaucer)			
Unto the pure all things are pure	Titus	Ch.1	v.15
Let your yea be yea; and your nay, nay	James	Ch.5	v.12
Ye have heard of the *patience of Job* (Also Chaucer)	James	Ch.5	v.11

As unto the *weaker vessel*	I Peter	Ch.3	v.7
Charity shall *cover a multitude of sins*	I Peter	Ch.4	v.8
The devil, as roaring lion, *seeking whom he may*			
devour	I Peter	Ch.5	v.8
His hairs . . . were as *white as snow*	Revelation	Ch.1	v.14
He shall rule them with a *rod of iron*	Revelation	Ch.2	v.27
. . . standing on the four corners of the earth	Revelation	Ch.7	v.1
. . . and he opened the *bottomless pit*	Revelation	Ch.9	v.2
. . . a pure river of the water of life, *clear as a*			
crystal	Revelation	Ch.22	v.1

The undermentioned words also occur in the bible, some more than once:

ado	stripling	craftiness	puffed up
Babbler and babblings (from Tower of Babel in Genesis)			long suffering
suburbs	leeks	backbiting	cornerstone
purloining	fellow	peep	cracknels
Shibboleth	mutter	oversight	jangling
shekels	outlandish	mortgaged	fainthearted
cucumber	brotherly love	backsliding	motheaten
beyond measure	covered wagons	no jot or tittle	byword
the inner man	tinkling	busybodies	anathema
brawlers	wrinkle	ringleader	tattlers
fire and brimstone		taskmaster	

This collection of words and expressions from the authorised (King James I) version of the Holy Bible is intended to show how many we still use in our daily parlance. Many have been varied or shortened in course of time, but the poetry of the Elizabethan translators shines through. Most of them are so apt that they remain unaltered.

A similar distillation from the plays of Shakespeare reveals several items also in the Bible. He would have been writing them during the period when other leading men of letters were at work on the Bible. Perhaps they borrowed from each other and all shared in England's golden age of literature.

Part III

Milton and Other Writers of the Past

SELECTIONS FROM MILTON, DICKENS, POPE, PEPYS AND OTHER WRITERS IN THE PAST

The expressions in this section were distilled from some 750 taken from works and anthologies from poets and writers in general: those chosen have an element of surprise on account of their origin in antiquity or who coined them.

Some of the expressions used by Dickens in his nineteenth-century novels can be traced back to early writers; but, although not originally his, it was because Dickens' novels were so widely read and his lectures so well attended that these expressions became cemented into our language.

It is interesting that, a century later, P G Wodehouse frequently included quotations from Shakespeare and the Bible in his writing. Although he used quotation marks, he did not always mention the writer's name and on these occasions Bertie Wooster always attributed the remark as coming directly from Jeeves (who else?!)

In Samuel Pepys famous and fascinating diary, which he never expected to be revealed, he used words and expressions which were surprisingly active over three centuries ago. Pepys also used a little 'Franglais' to veil his naughtiness.

It is debatable whether some familiar phrases were launched into our language by the classical philosophers or by their medieval translators - the choice is yours. In my view, Shakespeare remains supreme. A few well-worn quotations are included because people often use them to illustrate a point in their talk.

THE CLASSICS - 9TH CENTURY BC - AD 4TH CENTURY

CICERO (AD C1st)
He is his own worst enemy (*Ad Atticum* - also Sir T Browne, C17th)
Adding insult to injury (*Pro Tullio* - also E Moore, C18th)
While there's life there's hope (*Pro Tullio* - also J Gay, C18th)
Habit is a sort of *second nature* (*De Finibus*)
. . . the plough before the ox [the cart before the horse]

DELPHIC ORACLE [to Polycrates who asked for the whereabouts of hidden treasure] (C5th BC)
Leave no stone unturned
Know thyself: nothing in excess

HOMER (C9th BC)
The issue is in the *laps of the gods* (*Iliad*)

HORACE (C1st BC)
Well begun is half done (*Epistles*)
The mountain brought forth a ridiculous mouse (*Hrs Poetica*)
Often a purple patch, to give it colour (*Hrs Poetica*)
There is a certain method in his madness (*Satires* - also Shakespeare)

JUVENAL (AD C1st)
. . . a sound mind in a sound body (*Satires*)
The people long for just two things - *bread and circuses* (*Satires*)
At Rome, all things can be had *at a price* (*Satires*)

DIOGENES LAERTIUS (AD C3rd)
There are two sides to every question (*Protagoras*)

LIVY (C1st BC)
Romans celebrated a *nine days'* feast for a *wonderful* event (*History*)

LUCRETIUS (C1st BC)
One man's meat is another's poison (*De Rerum Natura* - also O Dykes, C18th)

Part III

MARTIAL (AD C1st)
So near and yet so far

OVID (AD C1st)
The dropping rain hollows out stone (*Epistulae & Porto*)

PETRONIUS (C1st BC)
He has joined the great majority (*c. Trimalchionis*)

PHAEDRUS (AD C1st)
Things are not always what they seem (*Fables*)

PLANTUS (C2nd BC)
He whom the gods love dies young (*Bacchides*)
Seeing is believing (*Truculentus*)

PLINY (AD C1st)
Take with a grain of salt (*Natural History*)
Home is where the heart is (*Natural History*)
The absent know by a ringing in the ears that they are talked about (*Natural History*)
. . . in wine there is truth [in vino veritas] (*Natural History*)

PLUTARCH (AD C1st)
Another such victory and we are ruined (*Pyrrhus*)

ST AMBROSE (AD C4th)
When in Rome, live as Romans do [Advice to St Augustine]

SUETONIUS (C1st BC)
The die is cast [Julius Caesar, on crossing the Rubicon]
Make haste slowly [Augustus Caesar]

PUBILIUS SYRUS (1st BC)
He gives twice who gives promptly
Familiarity breeds contempt
Hammer the iron when it is glowing hot [quoted by Rabelais, C16th]

36

Some remedies are worse than the disease (*Maxims* - also P Massinger, C17th)

TERENCE (C2nd BC)
Fortune favours the brave (*Phormio*)
. . . each a law unto himself (*Phormio*)

TERTULLIAN (AD C2nd)
He that fights and runs away may live to fight another day (also O Goldsmith, C18th)

VIRGIL (C1st BC)
A snake lurks in the grass (*Eclogue*)
My hair stood on end (*Aeneid*)
Beware of Greeks bearing gifts (*Aeneid*)

AESOP'S FABLES

I am sure the grapes are sour
A dog in a manger
Don't count your chickens before they are hatched
The wolf in sheep's clothing
He killed the goose with golden eggs
The gods help them who help themselves (also Euripides 425 BC)

CHAUCER - 14TH CENTURY

Canterbury Tales
A monk uncloistered is a ere *fish out of water*
. . . as brown as is a berye
Dede as a Dornayle down was he fallen
For aye 'as busy as bees' been they
Iren is hoot men sholden smyte (strike while the iron is hot)
Reeve's Tale: So was their jolly *whistle* well *y-wet*
Canon's Yeoman's Tale: For better than never is late
The Merchant's Tale: Love is blind
The Prioress's Tale: Mordre wol out [Murder will out] (also Congreve, 17th Century)
The Knight's Tale: At the King's court - *each man for himself*
            Love is law unto itself
Wife of Bath's Tale: For to see and eke for to be seen
Reeve's Tale: Thurgh thikke and thurgh thynne (also Dryden)
The Miller's Tale: As bold as brass
            Out of sight is also out of mind
The Cook's Tale: . . . if I pull your leg
            Many a true word has been said in jest
The Man of Law's Prologue: To the poor all times are out of joint
The Monk's Tale: I am an ugly customer
The Wife of Bath's Tale: A knowing wife, if she is worth her salt
The Merchant's Tale: . . . and as true as steel
The Canon Yeoman's Prologue and Tale:
            People will always find it bitter sweet
            Some outlandish cloak by day
            They stink as will a goat
            And therefore take no umbrage, sir, I pray
            I'll pay you on the nail
            I have a powder here that cost the earth
            Had taken it all for gospel, right as rain
            . . . he took it slyly out, the filthy sod

Troilus & Crysede
It is not good a sleeping hound to wake

Part III

Thus maketh vertue of necessitee

One ear heard it, and at the other it went out (*Poor Richard*)
Diverse pathes laden diverse folk the righte way to Rome (*Astrolabe*)
... castles in Spain (*Romount of Rose*)

14TH CENTURY

E DESCHAMPS
Who will bell the cat? (*Le chat et les souris* - also W Langland)

EDWARD III
Let the boy win his spurs (re: Black Prince)

J GOWER
Between two stools lieth the fall (*Confessio Amantis*)

W LANGLAND
Like father, like son (*Piers Plowman*)

J WYCLIF
By hook or by crook (*Tracts*)

15TH CENTURY

ANON
From Pillar to Post (Proverb)[1]

T HOCCLEVE
The pot so long to the water goeth, that home it cometh to the last y-broke (*De Regimine Principum*)

J LYDGATE
. . . as ballid [bald] as a cote [coot] (*Troy Book* - also R Burton)

SIR T MORE
They lepe lyke a flounder out of the fryinge panne into the fyre (*Heresy* - also J Heywood, Cervantes)
It was neither *rhyme nor reason* (*Apophthegms*)

16TH CENTURY

ANON
... his wits are *wool gathering*[2]
... to put a spoke in his wheel[3]
Tomorrow is another day (*Phyllida's Love Call*)

ARIOSTO
... fishing in troubled waters (*Orlando Furioso*)

T BECON
When the wine is in, the wit is out (*Catechism*)

J BRADFORD
But for the *grace of God*, there goes John Bradford (*Executions*)

DU BARTAS
Living from hand to mouth (*Divine Workes*)

ERASMUS
Talk of the devil and he'll appear (*Adagio*)

QUEEN ELIZABETH I

... who seeketh two strings to one bowe (to James VI)

J FLORIO
He robbeth Peter to pay Paul (*Firste Fruites*)[4]

SIR J FORTESCUE
Comparisons are odious (*De Laudibus Legum Angliae*)

R HANSARD
... to shew the number of his slaine enemys by the number of *fethers in his cappe*
(*History of Hungary*)

J & T HEYWOOD (*Proverbs*)

Beggars should be no choosers
She looks as butter would not melt in her mouth
A cat may look on a King
I know on which side my bread is buttered
New brome swepth cleene
Enough is as good as a feast
Two heads are better than one
One swallow maketh not summer
. . . might have gone further and fared worse
Anything for a quiet life (*The Captives* - also Dickens)

T INGELAND
None is so deaf as who will not hear (*Disobedient Child*)

MARTIN LUTHER
Who loves not wine, women and song remains a fool [Wer nicht liebt wein, weib und gesang, der bliebt ein narr]

J LYLY
No great smoke arises but there must be some fire (*Euphues*)
You goe about to *currey favour* (*Euphues*)
There is no fool like an old fool (*Mother Bombie*)

SIR J MELVILLE
Salt to Dysart or *coals to Newcastle* (*Autobiography*)

SIR T OVERBURY
The beauty of my wife *is but skin deep* (*A wife*)

RABELAIS (*Pamierge*)
The flea that I have in my ear
He always looked a given horse in the mouth (also S Butler)
. . . a baker's dozen
Plain as a nose in a man's face
Half the world knoweth not how the other half liveth

H ROBERT

Hold with the hare and run with the hounds (*Complaint*)

T SACKVILLE, EARL OF DORSET
His withered fist - *knocking at death's door* (*Miroure for Magistrates*)

SIR PHILIP SIDNEY
My dear, *my better half* (*Arcadia*)

E SPENSER
Though last, not least (*Colin Clout*)
A cruel crafty *crocodile* which in false grief - sheddeth tender tears (*Faerie Queen*)

G WHETSTONE
Birds of a fether, best flye together (*Promos & Cassandra*)

N WOODS
One bird in the hand is worth two in the bush (also Plutarch)

16TH/17TH CENTURY

ANON
The very streets are *paved with gold* (*New Jerusalem*)

BEAUMONT & FLETCHER
Kiss till the cow come home (*Scornful Lady*)
. . . be short and sweet (*Scornful Lady*)
The Devil take the hindmost (*Bonduca*)
Hit the nail on the head (*Love's Cure*)
One good turn deserves another (*Little French Lawyer*)

A BEHN
We are here today and gone tomorrow (*The Lucky Chance*)

BOOK OF COMMON PRAYER
Read, mark, learn and inwardly digest
Being now come to *years of discretion*
The iron entered his soul

SIR T BROWNE
Charity begins at home (*Religio Medici*)

J BUNYAN
The name of the *slough of despond* (*Pilgrim's Progress*)

S BUTLER
I smell a rat (*Hudibras*)
. . . have always been a *daggers drawn* (*Hudibras*)
. . . he knew *what's what* (*Hudibras*)

W CAMDEN
Better halfe a loafe than no bread (*Remains*)
The early bird catches the worm (*Remains*)
It is hard to teach an old dog new tricks (*Remains*)
Set a beggar on horseback (*Remains*)

CERVANTES
I have my own fish to fry (*Don Quixote*)
An honest man's word is as good as his bond (*Don Quixote*)
Not . . . all his eggs in one basket (*Don Quixote*)
Honesty is the best policy (*Don Quixote*)
Forewarned is foreared (*Don Quixote*)
As well look for a needle in a bottle of hay (*Don Quixote*)[5]
There are only two families in the world;
       the haves and the have nots (*Don Quixote*)
Thou hast seen nothing yet (*Don Quixote*)
Born with a silver spoon in his mouth (*Don Quixote*)
The proof of the pudding is in the eating (*Don Quixote*)
Thank you for nothing (*Don Quixote*)
Misfortunes seldom come singly (*Don Quixote*)
It will all come out in the wash (*Don Quixote*)
Let the worst come to the worst (*Don Quixote*)
Every dog has his day (*Don Quixote*)

CHRISTCHURCH MANUSCRIPT
All's set at *six and seven* (*Preparation* - also Shakespeare)[6]
The rolling stone can gather no moss (*Preparation*)

E COKE
. . . a man's house is his castle (*Institutes*)

W CONGREVE
Music hath charms to soothe the savage breast (*Mourning Bride*)
Hell hath no fury like a woman scorned (*Mourning Bride*)

DAVISON'S POETICAL RHAPSODY 1602
Absence makes the heart grow fonder

J DENNIS
Damn them . . . they *steal my thunder* (Stage effects)[7]

J DONNE
Comparisons are odious (*Elegies*)

No man is an island (*Devotions*)

GASCOIGNE
. . . and *popped a question for the nonce*

T HOBBES
. . . a great leap in the dark (*Last Words*)

C MARLOWE
I will make thee *beds of roses*

MICHEL DE MONTAIGNE
Few men are admired by their servants (*Essays*)
One foot in the grave (*Essays*)

J SELDEN
Preachers say: Do as I say, not as I do (*Table Talk*)
Throw a straw into the air - see which way the wind is (*Table Talk*)

SPINOZA
Nature abhors a vacuum [Latin Proverb] (*Ethics*)

DUC DE SULLY
The English take their pleasures sadly (*Memoirs*)

J TAYLOR
'Tis a mad world, my masters (*Western Voyage* - also Nicholas Breton)

T TUSSER
. . . a pig in a poke (*Good Husbandry*)[8]

WILLIAM III
I will die in *the last ditch*

MILTON - 17TH CENTURY

Paradise Lost
... of *Pandemonium*, proud city of Lucifer
... confusion worse confounded
... as built with *second thoughts*
... to invade *vacant possession*
... like the *weather-beaten* vessel (also T Campion)
A Heaven on Earth
Left him ... to his *dark designs*
... my *umpire*, Conscience
Wherefore ... *all hell broke loose*
... though *fallen on evil days*
... exactly to *thy heart's desire*
... beyond all bounds
... from all the ends of the Earth
A hideous *gabble* rises loud to see the *hubbub* strange

Paradise Regained
... governs the *inner man* (also Book of Common Prayer)
... argument of *human weakness*

Lycidas
Tomorrow to fresh *woods* and pastures new
Fame is the spur
How to scramble at the shearers' feast

Comus
Tipsy dance and jollity
... of Stygian darkness
There does a sable cloud turn forth her *silver lining*
And to the *tell-tale* sun descry
... *false alarms* of fear
Benighted walks under the *mid-day* sun
I was *all ear*

Samson Agonistes

. . . to live a *living death*
. . . and lorded over them
. . . adding fuel to the flame
. . . through the *high street* passing
Give us *eye-witness* of what was done
. . . of dire necessity (also Horace)
. . . calm of mind, *all passion spent*

On the *light fantastic* toe (*L'Allegro*)
Like one . . . *led astray* (*Il Penseroso*)
Sing *loud and clear* (*Psalm 81*)
. . . from *strength to strength* (*Psalm 84*)

SAMUEL PEPYS - C17th

1660

6 March	The dining-room was full of *tag, rag and bobtail,* dancing singing and drinking
25 March	by the same token . . .
1 June	The captain came on board . . . *quite fuddled.*
3 June	I will do you all the *good jobs* I can (Lord Sandwich)
5 July	. . . saw the King, the Dukes etc. go forth in the rain to the City and it *bedraggled* many a fine suit of clothes.

1661

7 November	I did not like his play, so I found a way *to put him off*
26 March	. . . which made their *mouths water*

1662

7 June	Mr. Coventry had already *feathered his nest* in the selling of places.

1663

6 January	It is *high time* to betake myself to my late vows
26 April	Tom, with whom I was angry for *botching* my camlott coat
1 May	I got out and kept myself *out of harm's way.*
27 May	a widow . . . sober and no *high-flyer*
23 June	but I do resolve even to let him go away for *good and all*
30 June	while Sir J. Minnes, like a dotard, *is led by the nose* by him.
20 October	I did give him a cuff or two *on the chops*; at last found him drunk.
21 October	bakers, butchers, brewers, draymen and *what-not*

1665

7 April	more money to be got for the navy or *we must shut up shop*
5 October	My mind is run *a wool gathering* and my business neglected
15 November	Lady Batten with new *spicke and span*

1666

28 January	Up, and being dressed, . . . took a *hackney coach* provided ready for me.[9]
10 May	A great deale of *tittle tattle* discourse to little purpose.

1667

11 June	Commissioner Pett, who is in a fearful *stink* for fear of the Dutch.
19 June	she come, and two of her *fellow-travellers* with her.
28 June	find my wife *making of tea*; a drink, which Mr. Pelling, the

51

pothicary, tells her is good for her cold.[10]

25 September I have not heard of one citizen *broke* in all this war, this plague, this fire.

25 September A play of Fletcher's which is but *so-so, methinks.*

10 October ... but I was *out of my wits* almost

11 November I had a whole doe sent me, and I had the *umbles* for dinner.[11]

1668

9 February ... which is to shut the door after the horse is stole

13 June ... (They) that live all seasons in these waters (at Bath) cannot but be *parboiled.*

4 November ... my coach ... carrying me to several places to do little jobs.

4 November The Duke of Buckingham *will not stop at anything.*

17TH CENTURY

F BACON
He that hath wife and children hath *given hostages to fortune* (*Marriage and Single Life*)

N BRETON
To rise with the lark (*Court and Country*)

R BROME
You rose on the wrong side of the bed (*Court Beggar*)

R BURTON
He . . . put his shoulder to the wheel (*Melancholy*)
Women wear the breeches (*Melancholy*)
If there is a *hell upon earth* (*Anatomy of Melancholy*)
. . . I call a spade a spade (*Anatomy of Melancholy*)
All his geese are swans (*Anatomy of Melancholy*)

W COWPER
. . . and they were *hand and glove* (*Retirement*)
Variety is the very spice of life (*Timepiece*)
The cups that cheer but not inebriate (*Winter Evening*)
Away went Gilpin neck or naught (*John Gilpin*)

SIR W DAVENPORT
I shall sleep like a top (*The Rivals*)

R FRANCK
Necessity is the mother of invention (*Northern Memoirs*)

T FULLER
Wilful waste brings woeful want (*Gnomologia*)
The load on *the willing horse* (*Gnomologia*)
From Hull, Hell and Halifax, Good Lord deliver us (*Yorkshire*)
It is always darkest just before the day dawneth (*Pisgah Sight*)

G HERBERT
The eye is bigger than the belly (*Jacula Prudentum*)
Whose house is of glass must not throw stones (*Jacula Prudentum*)
His bark is worse than his bite (*Jacula Prudentum*)
It is . . . *not worth the candle* (*Jacula Prudentum*)
Could'st thou both eat thy cake and have it? (*The Church*)

P HENRY
All this and heaven too!

T HERVEY
. . . are blessings in disguise (*Flower Garden*)

J HOWELL
All work and no play, makes Jack a dull boy (*Proverbs*)
A fool and his money are soon parted (*Familiar Letters*)
The spectator oft times sees more than the gamester (*Familiar Letters*)

EARL E HYDE
Peace at any price (*History of Rebellion*)

BEN JONSON
. . . who therein reaped *a just reward* (*Penshurst*)

F KLOPSTOCK
God and I knew . . . once; *now God alone knows*

SIR R L'ESTRANGE
We must practise what we preach (*Seneca's Morals* - also Chaucer)

R LOVELACE
Stone walls do not a prison make (*70 Althea*)

J RAY
He that hath many *irons in the fire*, some will cool (*Proverbs*)
Blood is thicker than water (*Proverbs*)
No man cries stinking fish (*Proverbs*)

The *last straw* breaks the camel's back (*Proverbs*)
I'll trust him no further than I can fling him (*Proverbs*)

P SCARRON
Send your *dirty linen* to the laundry (Don Juan d'Armenie)

J SHIRLEY
Take heed - *walls have ears* (Bird in a cage)

SIR J VANBRUGH
. . . 'tis much of a muchness (*Provoked Husband*)
He laughs best that laughs last (*The Country House*)

T WARD
The Hobson's choice - take that or none (*England's Reformation*)[12]

J WILSON
The exception proves the rule (*The Cheats*)

G WITHER
Little said is soonest mended (*The Shepherd Hunting* - also Chaucer)

A YARRANTON
There is no crying for shed milk (*England's Improvement*)

17TH/18TH CENTURY

H COWLEY
You must *mind your Ps and Qs* with him (*Who's the Dupe?*)

DRYDEN
. . . pimps for ill desires (*Absalom*)
Where infant punks their tender voices try (*Macflecknoe*)
Just at that point of time (*Macflecknoe*)

J GAY
Where there is life there's hope (*Beggar's Opera*)
Hath thy toil . . . consumed the *midnight oil*? (*The Shepherd and Philosopher*)
Sailors . . . in every port a mistress find (*Sweet William's Farewell*)

S RICHARDSON
It's a long lane that has no turning (*Clarissa Harlowe*)

J SWIFT
Receive the news in *doleful dumps* (on his death)
By spick and span I have enough (on his death)
In princes never put thy trust (on his death - also Psalm 146)
Furnishing . . . *sweetness and light* (*Battle of the Books*)
I heard a little bird say so (*Letter to Stella* - also Chaucer)
You have shot your bolt (*Polite Conversation*)
I won't keep a dog and bark myself (*Polite Conversation*)
The sight of you is good for sore eyes (*Polite Conversation*)
It would rain cats and dogs (*Polite Conversation*)
You can't make a silk purse out of a sow's ear (*Polite Conversation*)
A penny for your thoughts (*Polite Conversation*)

G VILLIERS
. . . now the plot thickens (on John Clifford)

VOLTAIRE
The embarrassment of riches (*Le Droit du Seigneur*)

POPE - 18TH CENTURY

Essay on Criticism
A little learning is a dangerous thing
To fetch and carry
To err is human; to forgive divine (quoting Seneca, AD 1st)
All looks yellow to the *jaundiced eye*
Fools rush in where angels fear to tread

Dr Arbuthnot
Damn with faint praise
Pride that *licks the dust*
The creature's at his *dirty work* again
Hope springs eternal in the human breast

Duncaid
Poetic Justice with her lifted scale
We bring to one *dead level* ev'ry mind

. . . and swept the board (*Rape of the Lock*)
. . . speed the parting guest (*Homer Odyssey 9th BC translation*)
The ruling passion (*Moral Essays*)
Do good by stealth (*Horace Satires 1st BC translation*)
. . . tempting with *forbidden fruit* (*Essay on Man*)

18TH CENTURY

T BROWN
What is sauce for the goose is sauce for the gander (*New Maxims*)

E BURKE
They will turn and bite the hand that fed them (*Scarcety*)
... a chip off the old block (*Pitt's Maiden Speech* - also W Rowley & Theocritus)
... the age of chivalry is gone (*French Revolution*)

F BURNEY/MADAME D'ARBLAY
Before you could say '*Jack Robinson*' (*Evelina* - also Sheridan)
... to take French leave (Diary 8 December 1782)[13]

R BURNS
Let us do or die (*Scots Wha-hae*)
... grew fast and furious (*Tam O'Shanter*)
The best-laid schemes ... gang aft agley (*To a Mouse*)
Don't let the *awkward squad* fire over me (*Cunningham*)

S BUTLER
... there's many a good tune played on an old fiddle (*Way of all flesh*)

C CHURCHILL
He'd *turn his nose up* at them all (*The Duellist*)

C CIBBER
This business *will never hold water* (*She Wou'd & Wou'd not*)
Perish that thought (*Richard III*)

W COLLINS
Twas sad *by fits, by starts* twas wild (*The Passions*)

W CONGREVE
Marry'd in haste, we may repent at leisure (*The Old Bachelor*)

W COWPER

Go the whole hog (*The Love of the World Reproved*)[14]

SIR H DUDLEY
Wonders will never cease (spoken to Garrick)

H FIELDING
I am as sober as a judge (*Don Quixote in England*)
Handsome is as handsome does (*Tom Jones*)

B FRANKLIN
. . . that man has an axe to grind
. . . as snug as a bug in a rug (*Advice to Young Traders*)
Remember that *time is money* (*Advice to Young Traders*)

O GOLDSMITH
The loud laugh that spoke *the vacant mind* (*Deserted Village*)
You may all *go to pot* (*Dinner at Dr Baker's*)
The very pink of perfection (*She Stoops to Conquer*)
The first blow is *half the battle* (*She Stoops to Conquer*)

T GRAY
. . . and waste its sweetness on the desert air (*Elegy*)
. . . some kindred spirit (*Elegy*)
. . . far from the madding crowd (*Elegy*)
It never rains but it pours (*Letter to Dr Wharton*)
Where ignorance is bliss, 'tis folly to be wise (*Eton College*)

DR JOHNSON
. . . but they are *necessary evils* (*Preface to Shakespeare*)
. . . no sooner does he take a pen in his hand than it becomes a torpedo to him (*Boswell*)[15]
Hell is paved with good intentions (*Boswell*)
When a man is to be hanged . . . it concentrates his mind wonderfully (*Boswell*)

R LE SAGE
. . . to burn the candle at both ends (*Gil Blas*)[16]

Part III

J O'KEEFE
. . . always except present company (*London Hermit*)

ROBESPIERRE
You can't make omelettes without breaking eggs

S ROGERS
You might have heard a pin drop (*Table Talk*)
Not dead, but gone before (*Human Life*)

ADAM SMITH
[England] . . . a nation of shopkeepers (*Wealth of Nations* - quoted by Napoleon)

SYDNEY SMITH
. . . a square person has squeezed himself into the round hole (*Square Pegs*)

T SMOLLET
. . . there is not enough room to swing a cat (*Humphrey Glinker*)
A fair exchange was no robbery (*Roderick Random*)
Make both ends meet (*Roderick Random*)

T SOUTHERNE
Revenge is sweet (*Sir Anthony Love*)

L STERNE
I'll not hurt a hair of thy head (*Tristram Shandy*)
'. . . what is this *story* about?' 'A *Cock and Bull*,' said Yorick (*Tristram Shandy*)
God tempers the wind to the shorn lamb (*Sentimental Journey*)

MARK TWAIN
Earning a precarious living by *taking in each other's washing*

J WESLEY
Cleanliness is, indeed, next to godliness (*On Dress*)

J WILKES
The chapter of accidents (*The Doctor*)

E YOUNG
Procrastination is the thief of time (*Night Thoughts*)

18TH/19TH CENTURY

E BULIVER-LYTTON
The pen is mightier than the sword (Richelieu)

T CAMPBELL
Like angel-visits, *few and far between* (*Pleasures of hope*)
Distance lends enchantment to the view (*Pleasures of hope*)
Coming events cast their shadows before (*Lochiel's Warning*)

S T COLERIDGE
With all the numberless *goings-on* of life (*Frost at Midnight*)
A sadder and a wiser man, he rose the morrow morn (*The Ancient Mariner*)

G COLMAN
. . . not to be sneezed at (*Heir-at-Law*)
His heart runs away with his head (*Who wants a Guinea*)
Give a dog an ill name and hang him (*Polly Honeycomb*)
No news is good news (*The Spleen*)

C LAMB
That illgotten gain (*Popular Fallacies*)

F MARRYAT
As savage as a *bear with a sore head* (*The King's Own*)
Let every man *paddle his own canoe* (*Settlers in Canada*)
It's just six of one and half a dozen of the other (*The Pirate*)

SAINTE-BEUVE
. . . as if in *his ivory tower* (*a' M Villemain*)

'SAM SLICK' (T C HALIBURTON)
Providence requires . . . *a stiff upper lip* (*Wise Saws*)
These men are all *upper crust* (*Wise Saws*)[17]
The Nelson Touch (*diary - 9.10.1805*)
. . . as large as life (*The Clockmaker*)

SIR W SCOTT
Fine words butter no parsnips (*Legend of Montrose*)
Tell that to the marines (*Redgarmtlet*)
To beard the lion in his den (*Marmion*)
The ancient pastime of *high jinks* (*Guy Mannering*)
Foemen worthy of their steel (*Lady of the Lake*)
... to see how the cat jumps (*Journal*)
... and nailed their colours to the mast (*Nelson, Pitt, Fox*)
... whirled them to the *back o'beyont* (*The Antiquary*)
There are as many good fish in the sea as ever came out of it (*Fortunes of Nigel*)

GENERAL SHERMAN
Hold the fort! I am coming (His message)

F E SMEDLEY
You are looking *as fresh as paint* (*Frank Fairclough*)
All's fair in love and war (*Frank Fairclough*)

TALLEYRAND
It is the beginning of the end (Napoleon's 1812 campaign)

W M THACKERAY
Them's my sentiments (*Vanity Fair*)
They have *a skeleton in their closet* (*The Newcombes*)

WELLINGTON
Our army is composed of the *scum of the earth*

DICKENS - C19th

A TALE OF TWO CITIES
. . . He'll always show *'em a clean pair of heels*
The jury retired under *watch and ward*
I am very much *put out* about my ladybird

BARNABY RUDGE
You'll find your father rather a *tough customer*
He will be a *cute* man yet[18]
"I do", said the 'prentice, "*Honour bright*".
It's as *plain as the nose on* Parkes's *face*
You made my *hair stand on end* and my *flesh creep*
. . . that *hangdog* face of yours, for hangdog it is
. . . all visitors *to cut and come again*, such a stupendous cheese!
Oh, very well, *if you're in a huff* . . .
It blows *great guns*
It gave me *such a turn* that you could *knock me down with a feather*
I am not much of *a dab* at my exercise
The sight of you is *good for sore eyes*
They might as well be *hanged for a sheep as a lamb*
They was as clear as a bell

BLEAK HOUSE
This is a *London Particular* [dense fog also known as Pea-souper][19]
What a load off my mind!
. . . galloping up hill and down dale
. . . not to put too fine a point upon it - *hard up*
The wind was in the east for three whole weeks [in bad temper]
. . . *requires a person to be wide awake* and have *his head screwed on tight*
He's too old to acquire the *knack* of it now
I shall devote my leisure to *moving heaven and earth* etc.
Volumnia is a little *dim*, . . . but of the true descent
Sir Leicester . . . moves among the company,
a magnificent *refrigerator*
. . . tumbled out *neck and crop* at a moment's notice
. . . a fearful *abortion* of a portrait of Sir Leicester

DAVID COPPERFIELD

a poor man, but as good as gold and true as steel
the boys in the school seemed to *send me to Coventry*[20]
. . . the wine shall be kept *to wet your whistle* [also Chaucer]
I was afraid that Steerforth would *twit* him with it
I am *rough*, sir, but I'm *ready*
I shall live in a perfectly new manner if - in short, anything *turns up*
. . . by way of anything that might be *on the cards*
Procrastination is the thief of time
. . . to look a gift horse in the mouth [to count its teeth for its age]
"Then", said Mr. Dick, "There'll be a *pretty kettle of fish.*"
A Suffolk Punch is *worth his weight in gold*[21]
. . . "in short, - *I'm floored*" (Mr. Micawber deep in debt)
. . . a grander kind of *going to the dogs*
"*Pays* as he speaks, my dear child, . . . *through his nose.*"
. . . a man who had been *born with a silver spoon*
. . . my nervous system must *have gone by the board*
I *fagged* through the park . . . long after *I felt quite knocked up*
Keep a good heart, sir! *never say die*, sir!
Let them the cap fitted, wear it
. . . There wasn't room to *swing a cat* there[22]
I must not be put upon
Britannia . . . is bound hand and foot with *red tape*
. . . being very anxious to *leave no stone unturned* [the Delphic Oracle]

DOMBEY AND SON

Florence was neglected in her dull *stately home*
Not while J.B. can *put a spoke in your wheel*, ma'am
If she *don't like* it, Mr. Dombey, she must be taught *to lump it*
He rose next morning *like a giant refreshed*
It ain't easy to break up *hearts of oak*
Mr. Carter rose *with the lark*
. . . and bring you on your *beam ends* with a lurch
Suddenly, like an *electric* shock, terror came upon him
She is no chicken

EDWIN DROOD
Don't *moddley-coddley*, there's a good fellow
You are very kind to join me . . . and *take pot luck*
Of such is the *salt of the earth* [Also Chaucer]
I might as well have *tried to wake the dead*
If you could *steal a march* upon a brigand . . . you had better do it
. . . as if he were falling into *a brown study*
I spent the night in *fits and starts*

GREAT EXPECTATIONS
. . . rolling in the *lap of luxury*
Well I'm *jiggered*!
. . . to hit a *happy medium between these two extremes*
Accidents will occur in the best regulated families
. . . "Your sister's *a master mind*"
Old Barley might be *as old as the hills* [Also Chaucer]
. . . we had it in a *twinkling*
. . . the ship's boys . . . *no longer fishing in troubled waters*
Find somebody with a little property . . . marry her *against a rainy day*
You great staring *stuck pig* [Also Chaucer]
He's going to ask the *whole gang*
. . . and we might as well *come well up to the mark*
You see *the millstone that is about my neck*
You're as *proud as Punch*, ain't you Aged?
I haven't been *so cut up* for a long time

HARD TIMES
You would *a' made no bones about it*
Why don't you *mind your own business?*

LITTLE DORRIT
Papa, potatoes, prunes and prisms are all very good words for the lips, especially prunes and prisms.

MARTIN CHUZZLEWIT
Money is the root of all evil
He looked *as if butter would not melt in his mouth*

Every man for himself
Such a bandying of words and calling of names
. . . born with *a silver spoon in my mouth*
"Some of us are *slow coaches*", said Mr. Pecksniff.
There's *a screw loose* in your affairs
You will have *to go farther - and to fare worse*
Is she so very *giddy* then?
Snap her up [Mrs. Gamp] *at any price.*
No objection to your *earning an honest penny*
She led her parent *the life of a dog*
'till he was *black in the face*
It *strikes me all of a heap*
He was as *mad* as a *march hare* [Also Chaucer]
It was the triumph of *mind over matter*
Tempted to *furnish forth* a pie [echo from Hamlet Act I]
His friend laughed heartily; Tom himself *was tickled.*
Leaves me high and dry without a leg to stand on
Not fit to *hold a candle to me*

NICHOLAS NICKLEBY
We don't *do thing bys halves* at our shop
A gentleman has a glass of punch before him - when another gent. comes and *collars* it.
. . . *the life and soul* of the Society
listening . . . with all *his might and main* [Also Chaucer]
The new [theatre] piece being a decided *hit*
No, not if *I work my fingers to the bone*
Ralph was *as deaf as an adder.*
An annuity would give you *a new lease of life*
She is come at last . . . and *all is gas and gaiters*
He clings to her apron strings
If you're in it *for a penny you're in it for a pound.*

OUR MUTUAL FRIEND
You that lodge in *Queer Street*
. . . laying the table cloth as if she were *raising the wind*
"No. 1 [secret]", said Bella, "will *electrify* you."

67

His flying off at a tangent
. . . the skeleton in the cupboard
Give a dog a bad name . . . and hang him
No, Bella, not one brass farthing.
My time being precious . . . *I'll make myself scarce.*

PICKWICK PAPERS
"Hush!" said Mr Jingle, *in a stage whisper.*
Every bullet has its billet
They went *at it tooth and nail*
"I say, old boy, where do you *hang out?*"
"He must be *a first-rater,*" said Sam. "*A 1*", replied Mrs. Roker.
"*Down upon your luck?* - *put that in his pipe.*"
No man should have more than two attachments - the first to *Number One* and
the second to the ladies.
I wants to *make your flesh creep*
Accidents will happen in the best regulated families
Never say die

OLIVER TWIST
Hard as nails
He knows *no more than the man in the moon*
Some divines do not always *practise what they preach*
Bring three dozen oysters and *look sharp about it.*
He *gives me the cold shoulder* on this very matter
. . . without ever *mincing of the matter* or *beating about the bush*
He would trespass on him for *a lift* [in a pony and cart]
Mr Swiveller, . . . accustomed to *sowing wild oats,* . . . considered that *half a loaf
is better than no bread.*

19TH CENTURY

M ARNOLD
Home of lost causes (Oxford)

J AUSTEN
. . . not turn a hair (Northanger Abbey)[23]

R H BARHAM
That's as clear as mud (*Ingoldsby Legends*)
There's many a slip twixt the cup and the lip (*Ingoldsby Legends*)
Here's the devil to pay! (*Hon. Mr Sucklethumbkin*)

W B BARNARD
. . . a Storm in a Teacup (Title of Play)

P T BARNHAM
There's a sucker born every minute

B BEE
There is Jackson, standing like a *stone wall* (*Bull Run*)

M BEERBOHM
I know nothing about music but I know what I like

R D BLACKMORE
All my eye and Betty Martin (*Perlycross*)

G BORROW
Youth will be served, every dog has his day (*Lavengro*)

H BRAISTED
She's not the only pebble on the beach (Title)

C BRONTE
. . . by a long chalk (*The Professor*)[24]

Part III

R BROWNING
. . . bear the brunt (*Prospice*)
A secret's safe *twixt you, me and the gate post* (*The Inn Album*)
. . . since he gave us the slip (*Waring*)

LORD BYRON
. . . truth is stranger than fiction (*Don Juan*)

M F CAREY
You can't keep a good man down (song title)

T CARLYLE
The iron hand in the velvet glove (*Latter-day Pamphlet*)
Silence is golden (*Sartor Resartus*)

L CARROLL
As large as life . . . (*Through the Looking Glass*)
As mad as a hatter (*Alice in Wonderland*)[25]

W COBBETT
You might have knocked me down with a feather (*Rural Rides*)

G CRABBE
. . . who cut and came again (*The Widow's Tale*)

J W CROKER
Heads I win, tails you lose (*Croker Papers*)

R H DANA
The captain, who knew the ropes (*Two years before the Mast*)

B DISRAELI
Their hearts are in the right place (*The Infernal Marriage*)
A dark horse, which had never been thought of (*The Duke)*

E DOWSON
Gone with the wind (*Cynara*)

A DUMAS PERE
Nothing succeeds like success (*Ange Pitou*)

R W EMERSON
In skating on thin ice, our safety is in our speed (*Essays*)

E FIELD
Listen to my *tale of woe* (*The Little Peach*)

GOETHE
Live dangerously and you live right (*Faust*)

LORD GOSCHEN
We have stood alone . . . in our *splendid isolation* (Speech 1896)

T HARDY
Prance as cats on hot bricks (*Necessitarian's Epitaph*)

T HUGHES
Life isn't all beer and skittles (*Tom Brown's Schooldays*)

M HUNGERFORD
Beauty is in the eye of the beholder (*Molly Brown*)

W IRVING
The almighty dollar . . . (*Wolfert's Roost*)

D JERROLD
We love peace . . . but *not peace at any price* (*Peace*)

C KINGSLEY
Helping lame dogs over stiles (letter to T Hughes)
It's fiddling while Rome is burning (*Westward Ho!*)

J KEATS
A thing of beauty is a joy for ever (*Endymion*)

71

A LINCOLN
It was not best to swap horses when crossing a stream

T LODGE
Devils are *not so black as they are painted* (*Margarite of America*)

LONGFELLOW
Don't cross the bridge till you come to it (*Golden Legend*)
Ships that pass in the night (*Tales of a Wayside Inn*)

J R LOWELL
I . . . go into it *baldheaded* (*The Biglow Papers*)

D MAIR
A bee in his bonnet (*Life of Mansie Waugh*)

G MEREDITH
Ah, what a *dusty answer* gets the soul (*Modern Love*)

T MORTON
Approbation from Sir Hubert Stanley is praise indeed (*A Cure for Heartache*)
What will *Mrs Grundy* say? (*Speed the Plough*)

T PAINE
From the sublime to the ridiculous . . . (*Napoleon's Retreat 1812*)

W PHILLIPS
Every man meets his Waterloo at last (Address to Press)

J R PLANCHE
. . . it would have made a cat laugh (*Queen of Frogs*)

T ROOSEVELT
The lunatic fringe . . . (*Autobiography*)

LORD JOHN RUSSELL
One provision . . . *was conspicuous by its absence* (speech)

SCHILLER
Live and let live (*Wallenstein's Camp*)

P B SHELLEY
Man . . . a traveller *from the cradle to the grave* (*Prometheus Unbound*)

R B SHERIDAN
I was struck all of a heap (*The Duenna*)

R SOUTHEY
. . . *agreed to differ* (*Life of Wesley*)
Curses . . . always *come home to roost* (*Curse of Kehama*)

R L STEVENSON
Don't make any bones about it (*St Ives*)

H B STOWE
He would sell me down the river (*Uncle Tom's Cabin*)

LORD TENNYSON
Airy, fairy Lilian (*Lilian*)
. . . for when *the time was ripe* (*Miller's Daughter*)
. . . the little rift within the lute (*Idylls of the King*)
Their's not to reason why (*Light Brigade*)
That strength . . . which moved *earth and heaven* (*Ulysses*)
Let us *hob and nob* with Death (*Vision of Sin*)

J WILSON
. . . born with a silver spoon in his mouth (*Noctes Ambrosianae*)
J WOLCOT
Care to our coffin adds a nail (*Expostulatory Odes*)

W WORDSWORTH
The river glideth *at his own sweet will* (*Upon Westminster Bridge*)

19TH/20TH CENTURY

R KIPLING
He travels fastest who travels alone (*The Winners*)
. . . the tail must wag the dog (*Conundrum of Workshops*)
. . . Little Tin Gods on Wheels (*Public Waste*)

20TH CENTURY

C J DENNIS
Me name is mud (*Sentimental Bloke*)

S GOLDWYN
In two words: im-possible
Include me out!

K GRAHAME
. . . messing about in boats (*Wind in the Willows*)

H DE C HASTINGS
A worm's eye view (*Architecture Review*)

I HAY
Funny peculiar or funny ha-ha (*The Housemaster*)

E PARAMORE
Hard-boiled as a picnic egg (*Yukon Jake*)

E PHILLPOTS
She had *bats in the belfry* and was put away (*Peacock House*)

LORD ROSEBERY
I must plough my furrow alone (speech)

D SAYERS
. . . spill the beans (*The Ballona Club*)

ST V TROUBRIDGE
There is an *iron curtain* across Europe (*Sunday News* - used by Winston Churchill at Fulton)

A WOOLCOTT
All the things I really like are immoral, illegal or fattening

NOTES

1. Probably from pillory to whipping post - to harry and to drive away vagabonds, etc., from one parish to another to avoid their charge upon parish funds.
2. Peasants, mostly children, combed the pastures to gather wool where sheep had rubbed against hedges, trees and fences. The reward was so little that only the simple-minded would take part.
3. In the sixteenth century, a spoke-pin was used to lock wheels on a slope.
4. This appeared very early in variations in Europe. In London it was supposed to derive from the refusal of the Dean of Westminster to take funds from St Peter's to maintain St Paul's.
5. Bottle = bundle
6. Two medieval Livery Companies in the City of London, The Skinners and The Merchant Taylors, were rivals to occupy the sixth place in the order of precedence among the Great Twelve. The strife between the two factions led to disorder and bloodshed in the streets. In consequence, the Mayor, Sir Robert Billesden, imposed the 'Billesden Award' upon both parties, declaring that each company would be sixth or seventh in alternate years. The reconciliation of the two companies in 1484 is depicted in a mural in the Royal Exchange. This 'alternation' continues to this day; but it still implies confusion. (Also mentioned in Shakespeare *Richard II*, Act II, scene ii)
7. John Dennis invented a device to simulate thunder for his play which failed in 1709. A few nights later it was used in Macbeth, whereupon he complained bitterly: 'they will not keep my play running, but they steal my thunder'.
8. Poke = sack, bag. Swindlers at medieval markets would offer a poke said to contain a piglet at a low price. When the buyer opened it at home a cat would leap out. If, however, it was opened on the spot 'the cat was out of the bag', thus giving the game away.
9. The coach horses were bred in *Hackney* Marshes near London and the name is still used on licences for vehicles for hire.
10. The mention of *tea* is well over 100 years before it became a popular refreshment using pots and cups with handles - hence 'a dish of tea'. Some people dried the leaves to spread on bread and butter.
11. 'umbles' - see Appendix 'Interesting Derivations': Dainty, humble, quarry.
12. The Cambridge hotelier, Hobson, used to hire out horses, but only of his own choosing. He told customers 'take that or none'.
13. In eighteenth-century France it was socially acceptable to quit a party without taking leave of the hostess. The British considered this to be rude or wicked and the term 'French Leave' implied desertion, absconding, absenteeism, etc. Fanny Burney married a French nobleman and became Mme D'Arblay.
14. Moslems were not sure which parts of the pig were forbidden, so they ate the lot.
15. Before the arrival of the naval weapon; Dr Johnson was referring to the ray fish of

sluggish habit.

16. Formerly, candles were fashioned in circular shape, like a horseshoe, to be lit at both ends.

17. The upper crust was considered to be the best part of the bread and was first offered to the aristocrats at the High Table.

18. Forebear of the Americanism?

19. This perennial handicap to traffic persisted until the middle of the twentieth century when the MP Sir Gerald Nabarro, brought in a bill to outlaw other than smokeless fuel to be used in the afflicted areas in the UK.

20. To send someone to Coventry means to refuse to speak to them.

21. Suffolk Punch = a shire horse

22. The cat referred to is not a pet but a thonged whip formerly used as a punishment in prisons and in the Navy.

23. To not turn a hair = to remain calm, unlike a horse whose hair is ruffled when he is distressed.

24. Refers to the use of chalk to score in games.

25. Early last century hatters worked with poisonous mercurial compounds in hat-making. The effects caused their gaits and speech to be clumsy and incoherent.

Shakespeare and Milton were comparatively near in time. John Milton was born in 1608 in Bread Street, Cheapside, where there was an entrance to the Mermaid Tavern, and as a child may well have seen William Shakespeare go by. He became a keen admirer of Shakespeare's writings, and while only twenty-two, wrote his famous epitaph to the great dramatist:

AN EPITAPH ON THE ADMIRABLE DRAMATIC POET, WILLIAM SHAKESPEARE

What needs my Shakespeare for his honoured bones,
The labour of an age in piled stones?
Or that his hallowed reliques should be hid
Under a star-y pointing pyramid?
Dear son of memory, great heir of fame,
What needst thou such weak witness of thy name?
Thou, in our wonder and astonishment,
Hast built thyself a live-long monument.
For whilst, to the shame of slow-endeavouring art,
Thy easy numbers flow; and that each heart

77

Part III

Hath, from the leaves of thy unvalued book,
Those Delphic lines with deep im0pression took;
Then thou, our fancy of itself bereaving,
Dost make us marble, with too much conceiving;
And so sepulchred, in such pomp dost lie,
That kings, for such a tomb, would wish to die.

JOHN MILTON

Part IV

Shakespeare

– The Highlights

from his 'Mirror up to Nature'

FOREWORD

This offering is a personal selection of the various facets which reveal Shakespeare's genius and his deep knowledge of human nature; but if readers prefer others – so much the better! Patient exploration of his writings will yield many more riches.

There appears among the plays the constant theme of the happy lot of the simple peasant compared with the burden of power, pomp and circumstance at court.

Shakespeare also teaches us how to behave (and how not to) in the fatal procrastination of Hamlet; the stubborn pride of Coriolanus; Othello's green-eyed monster' – jealousy; the turbulent temper of Lear; Macbeth's 'vaulting ambition'; and the vanity of Malvolio.

We are all there –
reflected in William's 'Magic Mirror!'

Charles Morrington

Member of 'The Queen's English Society'
Spring 1991

THE COMEDIES

THE TWO GENTLEMEN OF VERONA

THE TAMING OF THE SHREW

THE COMEDY OF ERRORS

LOVE'S LABOUR LOST

A MIDSUMMER-NIGHT'S DREAM

THE MERCHANT OF VENICE

THE MERRY WIVES OF WINDSOR

MUCH ADO ABOUT NOTHING

AS YOU LIKE IT

TWELFTH NIGHT

MEASURE FOR MEASURE

ALL'S WELL THAT ENDS WELL

THE WINTER'S TALE

THE TEMPEST

THE TWO GENTLEMEN OF VERONA

II, vii

Julia. The current that with gentle murmur glides,
   Thou know'st, being stopp'd, impatiently doth rage;
   But when his fair course is not hindered,
   He makes sweet music with the enamell'd stones,
   Giving a gentle kiss to every sedge
   He overtaketh in his pilgrimage;
   And so by many winding nooks he strays,
   With willing sport, to the wild ocean.
   Then let me go, and hinder not my course:
   I'll be as patient as a gentle stream,
   And make a pastime of each weary step,
   Till the last step have brought me to my love;
   And there I'll rest, as after much turmoil
   A blessed soul doth in Elysium.

III, ii

Proteus. As much as I can do, I will effect:
   But you, Sir Thurio, are not sharp enough;
   You must lay lime to tangle her desires
   By wailful sonnets, whose composed rhymes
   Should be full-fraught with serviceable vows.
Duke. Ay,
   Much is the force of heaven-bred poesy.
Proteus. Say that upon the altar of her beauty
   You sacrifice your tears, your sighs, your heart:
   Write till your ink be dry, and with your tears
   Moist it again; and frame some feeling line
   That may discover such integrity:
   For Orpheus' lute was strung with poets' sinews;
   Whose golden touch could soften steel and stones,
   Make tigers tame, and huge leviathans
   Forsake unsounded deeps to dance on sands.
   After your dire-lamenting elegies,

85

Part IV

Visit by night your lady's chamber-window
With some sweet consort; to their instruments
Tune a deploring dump: the night's dead silence
Will well become such sweet-complaining grievance.
This, or else nothing, will inherit her.[1]
(Shakespeare's advice to a timid lover)

THE TAMING OF THE SHREW

Introduction ii

Lord. Hence comes it that your kindred shuns your house, . . .
    O, noble lord, bethink thee of thy birth,
    Call home thy ancient thoughts from banishment,
    And banish hence these abject lowly dreams . . .
    Wilt thou have music? hark! Apollo plays,
    And twenty caged nightingales do sing: . . .
    Or wilt thou ride? thy horses shall be trapp'd,
    Their harness studded all with gold and pearl.
    Dost thou love hawking? thou hast hawks will soar
    Above the morning lark: or wilt thou hunt?
    Thy hounds shall make the welkin answer them,
    And fetch shrill echoes from the hollow earth.
1st Servant. Say thou wilt course, thy greyhounds are as swift
    As breathed stags, ay, fleeter than the roe.
2nd Servant. Dost thou love pictures? we will fetch thee straight
    Adonis painted by a running brook,
    And Cytherea all in sedges hid
    Which seem to move and wanton with her breath
    Even as the waving sedges play with wind.

I, ii

Petruchio. Why came I hither but to that intent?
    Think you a little din can daunt my ears?
    Have I not in my time heard lions roar?
    Have I not heard the sea puff'd up with winds
    Rage like an angry boar chafed with sweat?

86

Have I not heard great ordnance in the field,
And heaven's artillery thunder in the skies?
Have I not in a pitched battle heard
Loud 'larums, neighing steeds, and trumpets' clang:
And do you tell me of a woman's tongue
That gives not half so great a blow to hear
As will a chestnut in a farmer's fire?

IV, iii

Petruchio. Well, come, my Kate; we will unto your father's
Even in these honest mean habiliments:
Our purses shall be proud, our garments poor;
For 'tis the mind that makes the body rich;
And as the sun breaks through the darkest clouds,
So honour peereth in the meanest habit.
What, is the jay more precious than the lark,
Because his feathers are more beautiful?
Or is the adder better than the eel,
Because his painted skin contents the eye?
O, no, good Kate; neither art thou the worse
For this poor furniture and mean array.

V, ii

Katherine. Fie, fie! unknit that threatening unkind brow
And dart not scornful glances from those eyes,
To wound thy lord, thy king, thy governor:
It blots thy beauty as frosts do bite the meads,
Confounds thy fame as whirlwinds shake fair buds,
And in no sense is meet or amiable.
A woman moved is like a fountain troubled,
Muddy, ill-seeming, thick, bereft of beauty;
And while it is so, none so dry or thirsty
Will deign to sip or touch one drop of it.
Thy husband is thy lord, thy life, thy keeper,
Thy head, thy sovereign; one that cares for thee,
And for thy maintenance commits his body
To painful labour both by sea and land,

To watch the night in storms, the day in cold,
Whilst thou liest warm at home, secure and safe:
And craves no other tribute at thy hands
But love, fair looks and true obedience;
Too little payment for so great a debt.

A COMEDY OF ERRORS

II, i

Luciana.There's nothing situate under heaven's eye
  But hath his bound, in earth, in sea, in sky:
  The beasts, the fishes, and the winged fowls,
  Are their males' subjects and at their controls:
  Men more divine, the masters of all these,
  Lords of the wide world and wild watery seas,
  Indued with intellectual sense and souls,
  Of more pre-eminence than fish or fowls,
  Are masters to their females, and their lords:
  Then let your will attend on their accords.

LOVE'S LABOUR LOST

II, i

Princess. Good Lord Boyet, my beauty, though but mean,
  Needs not the painted flourish of your praise:
  Beauty is bought by judgement of the eye,
  Not utter'd by base sale of chapmen's tongues:
  I am less proud to hear you tell my worth
  Than you much willing to be counted wise
  In spending your wit in the praise of mine.

III, i

Biron. And I, forsooth, in love! I, that have been love's whip;

A very beadle to a humorous sigh;
A critic, nay, a night-watch constable;
A domineering pedant o'er the boy;
Than whom no mortal so magnificent!
This wimpled, whining, purblind, wayward boy;
This senior-junior, giant-dwarf Dan Cupid;
Regent of love-rhymes, lord of folded arms,
The anointed sovereign of sighs and groans, . . .

IV, iii

Have at you, then, affection's men at arms . . .
For when would you, my Lord, or you, or you,
Have found the ground of study's excellence
Without the beauty of a woman's face? . . .
But love, first learned in a lady's eyes,
Lives not alone immured in the brain;
But, with the motion of all elements,
Courses as swift as thought in every power,
And gives to every power a double power,
Above their functions and their offices.
It adds a precious seeing to the eye;
A lover's eyes will gaze an eagle blind;
A lover's ear will hear the lowest sound,
When the suspicious head of theft is stopp'd;
Love's feeling is more soft and sensible
Than are the tender horns of cockled snails;
Love's tongue proves dainty Bacchus gross in taste:
For valour, is not Love a Hercules,
Still climbing trees in the Hesperides?
Subtle as Sphinx; as sweet and musical
As bright Apollo's lute, strung with his hair;
And when Love speaks, the voice of all the gods
Makes heaven drowsy with the harmony.
Never durst poet touch a pen to write
Until his ink were temper'd with Love's sighs;
O, then his lines would ravage savage ears,
And plant in tyrants mild humility.

From women's eyes this doctrine I derive;
They sparkle still the right Promethean fire;
They are the books, the arts, the academes,
That show, contain and nourish all the world:
Else none at all in aught proves excellent.

V, ii

Rosaline. A jest's prosperity lies in the ear
Of him that hears it, never in the tongue
Of him that makes it:

A MIDSUMMER NIGHT'S DREAM

I, i

Theseus. Either to die the death, or to abjure
For ever the society of men,
Therefore, fair Hermia, question your desires;
Know of your youth, examine well your blood,
Whether, if you yield not to your father's choice,
You can endure the livery of a nun;
For aye to be in shady cloister mew'd,
To live a barren sister all your life,
Chanting faint hymns to the cold fruitless moon.
Thrice-blessed they that master so their blood,
To undergo such maiden pilgrimage;
But earthlier happy is the rose distill'd,
Than that which, withering on the virgin thorn,
Grows, lives, and dies in single blessedness.

II, ii

Titania. These are the forgeries of jealousy:
And never, since the middle summer's spring,
Met we on hill, in dale, forest or mead,
By paved fountain or by rushy brook,
Or in the beached margent of the sea,

To dance our ringlets to the whistling wind,
But with thy brawls thou hast disturb'd our sport.
Therefore the winds, piping to us in vain,
As in revenge, have suck'd up from the sea
Contagious fogs; which, falling in the land,
Have every pelting river made so proud,
That they have overborne their continents:
The ox hath therefore stretch'd his yoke in vain,
The ploughman lost his sweat; and the green corn
Hath rotted ere his youth attain'd a beard:
The fold stands empty in the drowned field,
And crows are fatted with the murrion flock;
The nine men's morris is fill'd up with mud;
And the quaint mazes in the wanton green,
For lack of tread, are undistinguishable;
The human mortals want their winter here;
No night is now with hymn or carol blest:
Therefore the moon, the governess of floods,
Pale in her anger, washes all the air,
That rheumatic diseases do abound:
And thorough this distemperature we see
The seasons alter: hoary-headed frosts
Fall in the fresh lap of the crimson rose;
And on old Hiems' thin and icy crown
An odorous chaplet of sweet summer buds
Is, as in mockery, set: the spring, the summer,
The chiding autumn, angry winter, change
Their wonted liveries; and the mazed world,
By their increase, now knows not which is which:
And this same progeny of evils comes
From our debate, from our dissension:
We are their parents and original.

Oberon. My gentle Puck, come hither. Thou rememberest
Since once I sat upon a promontory,
And heard a mermaid, on a dolphin's back,
Uttering such dulcet and harmonious breath,

That the rude sea grew civil at her song,
And certain stars shot madly from their spheres,
To hear the sea-maid's music . . .
That very time I saw, but thou couldst not,
Flying between the cold moon and the earth,
Cupid all arm'd: a certain aim he took
At a fair vestal throned by the west,
And loosed his love-shaft smartly from his bow,
As it should pierce a hundred thousand hearts:
But I might see young Cupid's fiery shaft
Quench'd in the chaste beams of the watery moon,
And the imperial votaress passed on
In maiden meditation fancy-free.
Yet mark'd I where the bolt of Cupid fell:
It fell upon a little western flower,
Before milk-white, now purple with love's wound,
And maidens call it love-in-idleness.

Oberon. I know a bank where the wild thyme blows,
Where oxlips and the nodding violet grows;
Quite over-canopied with luscious woodbine,
With sweet musk-roses, and with eglantine:
There sleeps Titania sometime of the night,
Lull'd in these flowers with dances and delight;
And there the snake throws her enamell'd skin,
Weed wide enough to wrap a fairy in:

V, i

Theseus. The lunatic, the lover and the poet
Are of imagination all compact:
One sees more devils than vast hell can hold,
That is the madman: the lover, all as frantic,
Sees Helen's beauty in the brow of Egypt:
The poet's eye in a fine frenzy rolling,
Doth glance from heaven to earth, from earth to heaven;
And as imagination bodies forth
The forms of things unknown, the poet's pen

Turns them to shapes, and gives to airy nothing
A local habitation and a name.

Theseus. I will hear that play;
    For never any thing can be amiss,
    When simpleness and duty tender it.
Theseus. Where I have come, great clerks have purposed
    To greet me with premeditated welcomes;
    Where I have seen them shiver and look pale,
    Make periods in the midst of sentences,
    Throttle their practised accents in their fears,
    And, in conclusion, dumbly have broke off,
    Not paying me a welcome. Trust me, sweet,
    Out of this silence yet I picked a welcome;
    And in the modesty of fearful duty
    I read as much as from the rattling tongue
    Of saucy and audacious eloquence.
    Love, therefore, and tongue-tied simplicity
    In least speak most, to my capacity.

Theseus. The iron tongue of midnight hath told twelve:
    Lovers, to bed; 'tis almost fairy time.
    I fear we shall out-sleep the coming morn,
    As much as we this night have overwatch'd.
    This palpable-gross play hath well beguiled
    The heavy gait of night. Sweet friends, to bed.

THE MERCHANT OF VENICE

I, i

Bassanio. In Belmont is a lady richly left;
    And she is fair, and, fairer than that word,
    Of wondrous virtues: sometimes from her eyes
    I did receive fair speechless messages:
    Her name is Portia; nothing undervalued

To Cato's daughter, Brutus' Portia:
Nor is the wide world ignorant of her worth;
For the four winds blow in from every coast
Renowned suitors: and her sunny locks
Hang on her temples like a golden fleece;
Which makes her seat of Belmont Colchos' strond,
And many Jasons come in quest of her.

I, iii

Shylock. Signor Antonio, many a time and oft
  In the Rialto you have rated me
  About my moneys and my usances:
  Still have I borne it with a patient shrug;
  For sufferance is the badge of all our tribe.
  You call me misbeliever, cut-throat dog,
  And spit upon my Jewish gaberdine,
  And all for use of that which is mine own.
  Well then it now appears you need my help:
  Go to, then: you come to me, and you say
  'Shylock, we would have moneys:' you say so;
  You, that did void your rheum upon my beard,
  And foot me as you spurn a stranger cur
  Over your threshold: moneys is your suit.
  What should I say to you? Should I not say
  'Hath a dog money? is it possible
  A cur can lend three thousand ducats?' or
  Shall I bend low and in a bondman's key,
  With bated breath and whispering humbleness,
  Say this, -
  'Fair sir, you spit on me on Wednesday last;
  You spurn'd me such a day; another time
  You call'd me dog; and for these courtesies
  I'll lend you thus much moneys'?

II, i

Morocco. Mislike me not for my complexion,
  The shadow'd livery of the burnish'd sun,

To whom I am a neighbour and near bred.
Bring me the fairest creature northward born,
Where Phoebus' fire scarce thaws the icicles,
And let us make incision for your love,
To prove whose blood is reddest, his or mine,
I tell thee, lady, this aspect of mine
Hath fear'd the valiant: by my love, I swear
The best-regarded virgins of our clime
Have loved it too: I would not change this hue,
Except to steal your thoughts, my gentle queen.

II, vi

. . .
Gratiano. That ever holds: who riseth from a feast
    With that keen appetite that he sits down?
    Where is the horse that doth untread again
    His tedious measures with the unbated fire
    That he did pace them first? All things that are,
    Are with more spirit chased than enjoy'd,
    How like a younker or a prodigal
    The scarfed bark puts from her native bay
    Hugg'd and embraced by the strumpet wind!
    How like the prodigal doth she return,
    With over-weather'd ribs and ragged sails,
    Lean, rent, and beggar'd by the strumpet wind!

IV, i

Portia. The quality of mercy is not strain'd,
    It droppeth as the gentle rain from heaven
    Upon the place beneath; it is twice blest;
    It blesseth him that gives, and him that takes:
    'Tis mightiest in the mightiest: it becomes
    The throned monarch better than his crown;
    His sceptre shows the force of temporal power,
    The attribute to awe and majesty,
    Wherein doth sit the dread and fear of kings;
    But mercy is above its sceptred sway;

It is enthroned in the hearts of kings,
It is an attribute to God himself;
And earthly power doth then show likest God's
When mercy seasons justice.

V, i

Lorenzo. The moon shines bright: in such a night as this,
    When the sweet wind did gently kiss the trees
    And they did make no noise, in such a night
    Troilus methinks mounted the Troyan walls,
    And sigh'd his soul toward the Grecian tents,
    Where Cressid lay that night.
Jessica. In such a night
    Did Thisbe fearfully o'ertrip the dew,
    And saw the lion's shadow ere himself
    And ran dismay'd away.
Lorenzo. In such a night
    Stood Dido with a willow in her hand
    Upon the wild sea banks, and waft her love
    To come again to Carthage.
Jessica. In such a night
    Medea gather'd the enchanted herbs
    That did renew old Aeson.

Lorenzo. How sweet the moonlight sleeps upon this bank!
    Here will we sit, and let the sounds of music
    Creep in our ears: soft stillness and the night
    Become the touches of sweet harmony.
    Sit, Jessica. Look how the floor of heaven
    Is thick inlaid with patines of bright gold:
    There's not the smallest orb which thou behold'st
    But in his motion like an angel sings,
    Still quiring to the young-eyed cherubins;
    Such harmony is in immortal souls; . . .

Jessica. I am never merry when I hear sweet music.
Lorenzo. The reason is, your spirits are attentive:

For do but note a wild and wanton herd,
Or race of youthful and unhandled colts,
Fetching mad bounds, bellowing and neighing loud,
Which is the hot condition of their blood;
If they but hear perchance a trumpet sound,
Or any air of music touch their ears,
You shall perceive them make a mutual stand,
Their savage eyes turn'd to a modest gaze
By the sweet power of music: therefore the poet
Did feign that Orpheus drew trees, stones and floods,
Since nought so stockish, hard and full of rage,
But music for the time doth change his nature.
The man that hath no music in himself,
Nor is not moved with concord of sweet sounds,
Is fit for treasons, stratagems and spoils;
And his affections dark as Erebus:
Let no such man be trusted. Mark the music.
                    (Enter Portia and Nerissa)
Portia. That light we see is burning in my hall.
    How far that little candle throws his beams!
    So shines a good deed in a naughty world.
Nerissa. When the moon shone, we did not see the candle.
Portia. So doth the greater glory dim the less:
    A substitute shines brightly as a king,
    Until a king be by; and then his state
    Empties itself, as doth an inland brook
    Into the main of waters. Music! hark!
Nerissa. It is your music, madam, of the house.
Portia. Nothing is good, I see, without respect:
    Methinks it sounds much sweeter than by day.
Nerissa. Silence bestows that virtue on it, madam.
Portia. The crow doth sing as sweetly as the lark,
    When neither is attended; and I think
    The nightingale, if she should sing by day,
    When every goose is cackling, would be thought
    No better a musician than the wren.
    How many things by season season'd are

97

To their right praise and true perfection!

THE MERRY WIVES OF WINDSOR

V, v

Mistress Quickly . . .
Search Windsor Castle, elves, within and out:
Strew good luck, ouphes, on every sacred room;
That it may stand till the perpetual doom, . . .
And nightly, meadow-fairies, look you sing,
Like to the Garter's compass, in a ring:
Th'expressure that it bears, green let it be,
More fertile-fresh than all the fields to see;
And 'Honi soit qui mal y pense' write
In emerald tufts, flowers purple, blue, and white;
Like sapphire, pearl, and rich embroidery,
Buckled below fair knighthood's bending knee:

MUCH ADO ABOUT NOTHING

V, iii

Don Pedro. Good morrow, masters; put your torches out:
The wolves have prey'd; and look, the gentle day,
Before the wheels of Phoebus, round about
Dapples the drowsy east with spots of grey.
Thanks to you all, and leave us: fare you well.

V, iv

Don Pedro. Good morrow, Benedick. Why, what's the matter,
That you have such a February face,
So full of frost, of storm, and cloudiness?

AS YOU LIKE IT

Orlando: Shall I keep your hogs and eat husks with them?
. . . What prodigal portion have I spent, that I should come to such penury?[2]

Duke S. Now, my co-mates and brothers in exile,
   Hath not old custom made this life more sweet
   Than that of painted pomp? Are not these woods
   More free from peril than the envious court?
   Here feel we but the penalty of Adam,
   The seasons' difference; as the icy fang
   And churlish chidings of the winter's wind,
   Which, when it bites and blows upon my body,
   Even till I shrink with cold, I smile and say
   'This is no flattery: these are counsellors
   That feelingly persuade me what I am.'
   Sweet are the uses of adversity;
   Which, like the toad, ugly and venomous,
   Wears yet a precious jewel in his head:
   And this our life exempt from public haunt
   Finds tongues in trees, books in running brooks,
   Sermons in stones and good in everything.

Adam . . . When service should in my old limbs lie lame,
   And unregarded age in corners thrown:
   Take that, and He that doth the ravens feed,
   Yea, providently caters for the sparrow,
   Be comfort to my age! . . . Let me be your servant:
   Though I look old, yet I am strong and lusty;
   For in my youth I never did apply
   Hot and rebellious liquors in my blood,
   Nor did not with unbashful forehead woo
   The means of weakness and debility;
   Therefore my age is as a lusty winter,

Frosty, but kindly: let me go with you:
I'll do the service of a younger man
In all your business and necessities.

II, vii

Orlando. Speak you so gently? Pardon me, I pray you:
   I thought that all things had been savage here;
   And therefore put I on the countenance
   Of stern commandment. But whate'er you are
   That in this desert inaccessible,
   Under the shade of melancholy boughs,
   Lose and neglect the creeping hours of time;
   If ever you have look'd on better days,
   If ever been where bells have knoll'd to church,
   If ever sat at any good man's feast,
   If ever from your eyelids wiped a tear
   And know what 'tis to pity and be pitied,
   Let gentleness my strong enforcement be:
   In the which hope I blush, and hide my sword.

Duke S. True is it that we have seen better days,
   And have with holy bell been knoll'd to church,
   And sat at good men's feasts, and wiped our eyes
   Of drops that sacred pity hath engender'd:
   And therefore sit you down in gentleness . . .

Orlando. Then but forbear your food a little while,
   Whiles, like a doe, I go to find my fawn
   And give it food.

Duke S. God find him out, . . .
   Thou seest we are not all alone unhappy:
   This wide and universal theatre
   Presents more woeful pageants than the scene
   Wherein we play in.

Jaques. All the world's a stage,

And all the men and women merely players:
They have their exits and their entrances;
And one man in his time plays many parts,
His acts being seven ages. At first the infant,
Mewling and puking in the nurse's arms.
Then the whining school-boy, with his satchel
And shining morning face, creeping like snail
Unwillingly to school. And then the lover,
Sighing like furnace, with a woeful ballad
Made to his mistress' eyebrow. Then a soldier,
Full of strange oaths, and bearded like the pard,
Jealous in honour, sudden and quick in quarrel,
Even in the cannon's mouth. And then the justice
In fair round belly with good capon lined,
With eyes severe and beard of formal cut,
Full of wise saws and modern instances:
And so he plays his part. The sixth age shifts
Into the lean and slipper'd pantaloon,
With spectacles on nose and pouch on side,
His youthful hose, well saved, a world too wide
For his shrunk shank; and his big manly voice,
Turning again toward childish treble, pipes
And whistles in his sound. Last scene of all,
That ends this strange eventful history,
Is second childishness and mere oblivion,
Sans teeth, sans eyes, sans taste, sans every thing.

TWELFTH NIGHT

I, i

Duke. If music be the food of love, play on;
　Give me excess of it, that, surfeiting,
　The appetite may sicken, and so die.
　That strain again! it had a dying fall:
　O, it came o'er my ear like the sweet sound

Part IV

That breathes upon a bank of violets
Stealing and giving odour!

I, v

Olivia. Why, what would you?
Viola. Make me a willow cabin at your gate,
  And call upon my soul within the house;
  Write loyal cantons of contemned love
  And sing them loud even in the dead of night;
  Halloo your name to the reverberate hills,
  And make the babbling gossip of the air
  Cry out 'Olivia!' O, you should not rest
  Between the elements of air and earth,
  But you should pity me!

Olivia. 'What is your parentage?'
  'Above my fortunes, yet my state is well:
  I am a gentleman.' - I'll be sworn thou art:
  Thy tongue, thy face, thy limbs, actions, and spirit,
  Do give thee five-fold blazon: not too fast: soft, soft!
  Unless the master were the man. How now!
  Even so quickly may one catch the plague?
  Methinks I feel this youth's perfections
  With an invisible and subtle stealth
  To creep in at my eyes.

II, iv

Duke. And what's her history?
Viola. A blank, my lord. She never told her love,
  But let concealment, like a worm i' the bud,
  Feed on her damask cheek: she pined in thought;
  And with a green and yellow melancholy
  She sat like patience on a monument,
  Smiling at grief. Was not this love indeed?

III, iv

Malvolio. 'Be not afraid of greatness:' 'twas well writ . . .

'Some are born great,' . . .
'Some achieve greatness,' . . .
'And some have greatness thrust upon them.'

MEASURE FOR MEASURE

II, i

Angelo. We must not make a scarecrow of the law,
  Setting it up to fear the birds of prey,
  And let it keep one shape, till custom make it
  Their perch and not their terror.

II, ii

Isabel. No ceremony that to great ones 'longs
  Not the king's crown, nor the deputed sword,
  The marshall's truncheon, nor the judge's robe,
  Become them with one half so good a grace
  As mercy does . . .
  Why, all the souls that were, were forfeit once;
  And He that might the vantage best have took
  Found out the remedy. How would you be,
  If He, which is the top of judgement, should
  But judge you as you are? O, think on that;
  And mercy then will breathe within your lips,
  Like man new made . . . Spare him, spare him!
  He's not prepared for death. Even for our kitchens
  We kill the fowl of season: shall we serve heaven
  With less respect than we do minister
  To our gross selves? . . .
  Could great men thunder
  As Jove himself does, Jove would ne'er be quiet,
  For every pelting, petty officer
  Would use his heaven for thunder! Merciful Heaven,
  Thou rather with thy sharp and sulphurous bolt
  Split'st the unwedgeable and gnarled oak

103

Than the soft myrtle: but man, proud man.
Drest in a little brief authority,
Most ignorant of what he's most assured,
His glassy essence, like an angry ape,
Plays such fantastic tricks before high heaven
As make the angels weep; . . .
Because authority, though it err like others,
Hath yet a kind of medicine in itself,
That skins the vice o' the top . . .
Hark how I'll bribe you:
. . . Not with fond sicles of the tested gold,
Or stones whose rates are either rich or poor
As fancy values them; but with true prayers
That shall be up at heaven and enter there
Ere sun-rise, prayers from preserved souls,
From fasting maids whose minds are dedicate
To nothing temporal.
Angelo. What's this, what's this? Is this her fault or mine?
The tempter or the tempted, who sins most?
Ha!
Not she; nor doth she tempt: but it is I
That, lying by the violet in the sun,
Do as the carrion does, not as the flower,
Corrupt with virtuous season. Can it be
That modesty may more betray our sense
Than woman's lightness? Having waste ground enough,
Shall we desire to raze the sanctuary,
And pitch our evils there? . . .
O, cunning enemy, that, to catch a saint,
With saints doth bait thy hook! Most dangerous
Is that temptation that doth goad us on
To sin in loving virtue: never could the strumpet,
With all her double vigour, art and nature,
Once stir my temper; but this virtuous maid
Subdues me quite. Ever till now,
When men were fond, I smiled, and wonder'd how.

Duke. Be absolute for death, either death or life
    Shall thereby be the sweeter. Reason thus with life:
    If I do lose thee I do lose a thing
    That none but fools would keep: a breath thou art,
    Servile to all the skyey influences,
    That dost this habitation, where thou keep'st,
    Hourly afflict: merely, thou art death's fool;
    For him thou labour'st by thy flight to shun,
    And yet runn'st toward him still. Thou art not noble;
    For all the accommodations that thou bear'st
    Are nursed by baseness. Thou'rt by no means valiant;
    For thou dost fear the soft and tender fork
    Of a poor worm. Thy best of rest is sleep,
    And that thou oft provokest; yet grossly fear'st
    Thy death, which is no more. Thou art not thyself;
    For thou exist'st on many a thousand grains
    That issue out of dust. Happy thou art not;
    For what thou hast not, still thou strivest to get,
    And what thou hast, forget'st. Thou art not certain;
    For thy complexion shifts to strange effects,
    After the moon. If thou art rich, thou'rt poor;
    For, like an ass whose back with ingots bows,
    Thou bear'st thy heavy riches but a journey,
    And death unloads thee. Friend hast thou none;
    For thine own bowels, which do call thee sire,
    The mere effusion of thy proper loins,
    Do curse the gout, serpigo, and the rheum;
    For ending you no sooner. Thou hast nor youth nor age,
    But, as it were, an after-dinner's sleep,
    Dreaming on both; for all thy blessed youth
    Becomes as aged, and doth beg the alms
    Of palsied eld; and when thou art old and rich,
    Thou hast neither heat, affection, limb, nor beauty,
    To make thy riches pleasant. What's yet in this
    That bears the name of life? Yet in this life
    Lie hid more thousand deaths: yet death we fear,

That makes these odds all even.

Claudio. Ay, but to die, and go we know not where;
To lie in cold obstruction and to rot;
This sensible warm motion to become
A kneaded clod; and the delighted spirit
To bathe in fiery floods, or to reside
In thrilling region of thick-ribbed ice;
To be imprison'd in the viewless winds,
And blown with restless violence round about
The pendent world; or to be worse than worst
Of those that lawless and incertain thought
Imagine howling:- 'tis too horrible!
The weariest and most loathed worldly life
That age, ache, penury, and imprisonment
Can lay on nature is a paradise
To what we fear in death.

ALL'S WELL THAT ENDS WELL

IV, iii

First Lord. The web of our life is of mingled yarn, good and ill together: our
virtues would be proud, if our faults whipped them not; and our crimes would
despair, if they were not cherished by our virtues.

Epilogue

King. The king's a beggar, now the play is done:
All is well ended, if this suit be won,
That you express content; which we will pay,
With strife to please you, day exceeding day:
Ours be your patience then, and yours our parts;
Your gentle hands lend us, and take our hearts.[4]
(The most endearing of Shakespeare's Epilogues)

THE WINTER'S TALE

Bohemia, a desert country near the sea.

III, 3

Antigonus: This is the chase: I am gone forever
    (Exit, pursued by a bear)[5]

IV, iv

Perdita. I'll not put
    The dibble in earth to set one slip of them; . . .
    Here's flowers for you;
    Hot lavender, mints, savory, marjoram;
    The marigold, that goes to bed wi' the sun
    And with him rises weeping: these are flowers of middle summer,
    And I think they are given to men of middle age . . .
    Now, my fair'st friend,
    I would I had some flowers o' the spring that might
    Become your time of day; . . . O, Proserpina,
    For the flowers now, that frighted thou let'st fall
    From Dis's waggon! daffodils,
    That come before the swallow dares, and take
    The winds of March with beauty; violets dim,
    But sweeter than the lids of Juno's eyes
    Or Cytherea's breath; pale primroses,
    That die unmarried, ere they can behold
    Bright Phoebus in his strength, a malady
    Most incident of maids; bold oxlips and
    The crown imperial: lilies of all kinds,
    The flower-de-luce being one! O, these I lack,
    To make you garlands of; and my sweet friend,
    To strew him o'er and o'er!

THE TEMPEST

Francisco . . .
    Sir, he may live:
I saw him beat the surges under him,
And ride upon their backs; he trod the water,
Whose enmity he flung aside, and breasted
The surge most swoln that met him; his bold head
'Bove the contentious waves he kept, and oar'd
Himself with his good arms in lusty stroke
To the shore, that o'er his wave-born basis bow'd,
As stooping to relieve him: I not doubt
He came alive to land:

Ferdinand . . .
                    Admired Miranda
Indeed the top of admiration! worth
What's dearest to the world! Full many a lady
I have eyed with best regard, and many a time
The harmony of their tongues hath into bondage
Brought my too diligent ear: for several virtues
Have I liked several women; never any
With so full soul, but some defect in her
Did quarrel with the noblest grace she owed,
And put it to the foil: but you, O you,
So perfect and so peerless, are created
Of every creature's best!

Caliban. Be not afeard; the isle is full of noises,
    Sounds and sweet airs, that give delight, and hurt not.
    Sometimes a thousand twangling instruments
    Will hum about mine ears; and sometimes voices
    That, if I then had waked after long sleep,
    Will make me sleep again: and then, in dreaming,

The clouds methought would open, and show riches
Ready to drop upon me: that, when I waked,
I cried to dream again.

IV, i

Prospero. You do look, my son, in a moved sort,
  As if you were dismay'd: be cheerful, sir.
  Our revels now are ended. These our actors,
  As I foretold you, were all spirits, and
  Are melted into air, into thin air:
  The cloud-capp'd towers, the gorgeous palaces,
  The solemn temples, the great globe itself,
  Yea, all which it inherit, shall dissolve,
  And, like this insubstantial pageant faded,
  Leave not a rack behind. We are such stuff
  As dreams are made on; and our little life
  Is rounded with a sleep.[7]

V i

Prospero. Ye elves of hills, brooks, standing lakes, and groves;
  And ye that on the sands with printless foot
  Do chase the ebbing Neptune, and do fly him
  When he comes back; you demi-puppets that
  By moonshine do the green sour ringlets make
  Whereof the ewe not bites; and you whose pastime
  Is to make midnight mushrooms, that rejoice
  To hear the solemn curfew; by whose aid -
  Weak masters though ye be - I have bedimm'd
  The noontide sun, call'd forth the mutinous winds,
  And 'twixt the green sea and the azured vault
  Set roaring war: to the dread rattling thunder
  Have I given fire, and rifted Jove's stout oak
  With his own bolt; the strong-based promontory
  Have I made shake, and by the spurs pluck'd up
  The pine and cedar: graves at my command
  Have waked their sleepers, oped, and let 'em forth
  By my so potent art. But this rough magic

I here abjure; and, when I have required
Some heavenly music, - which even now I do, -
To work mine end upon their senses, that,
This airy charm is for, I'll break my staff,
Bury it certain fathoms in the earth,
And deeper than did ever plummet sound
I'll drown my book.

SHAKESPEARE COMEDIES - NOTES

1. Shakespeare's advice to a timid lover
2. See St Luke's parable
3. One of Shakespeare's great speeches rich in philosophy and touching human nature
4. This is, perhaps, the most endearing of Shakespeare's epilogues
5. The most astonishing stage direction in the history of the theatre
6. Shakespeare's finest threnody
7. Shakespeare's farewell to the stage

...... and HIGHLIGHTS FROM THE TRAGEDIES

TROILUS AND CRESSIDA

ROMEO AND JULIET

JULIUS CAESAR

HAMLET, PRINCE OF DENMARK

OTHELLO

KING LEAR

MACBETH

ANTONY AND CLEOPATRA

CORIOLANUS

PERICLES, PRINCE OF TYRE

CYMBELINE

Shakespeare

TROILUS AND CRESSIDA

Ulysses to Achilles.

Time hath, my lord, a wallet at his back
Wherein he puts alms for oblivion,
A great-sized monster of ingratitudes:
Those scraps are good deeds past, which are devour'd
As fast as they are made, forgot as soon
As done: perseverance, dear my lord,
Keeps honour bright: to have done, is to hang
Quite out of fashion, like a rusty mail
In monumental mockery. Take the instant way;
For honour travels in a strait so narrow,
Where one but goes abreast: keep then the path;
For emulation hath a thousand sons
That one by one pursue: if you give way,
Or hedge aside from the direct forthright,
Like to an enter'd tide they all rush by
And leave you hindmost:
Or, like a gallant horse fall'n in first rank,
Lie there for pavement to the abject rear,
O'er-run and trampled on: then what they do in present,
Though less than yours in past, must o'ertop yours;
For time is like a fashionable host
That slightly shakes his parting guest by the hand,
And with his arms outstretch'd, as he would fly,
Grasps in the comer: welcome ever smiles,
And farewell goes out sighing. O, let not virtue seek
Remuneration for the thing it was;
For beauty, wit,
High birth, vigour of bone, desert in service,
Love, friendship, charity, are subjects all
To envious and calumniating time.
One touch of nature makes the whole world kin;
That all with one consent praise new-born gawds,

113

Though they are made and moulded of things past.
And give to dust that is a little gilt
More laud than gilt o'er-dusted.
The present eye praises the present object:
Then marvel not, thou great and complete man,
That all the Greeks begin to worship Ajax;
Since things in motion sooner catch the eye
Than what not stirs. The cry went once on thee,
And still it might, and yet it may again,
If thou would'st not entomb thyself alive
And case thy reputation in thy tent,
Whose glorious deeds, but in these fields of late,
Made emulous missions 'mongst the gods themselves
And drave great Mars to faction.[3]

(One of Shakespeare's great speeches, rich in philosophy and touching human nature.)

ROMEO AND JULIET

I, The Prologue

Chorus. Two households, both alike in dignity,
   In fair Verona, where we lay our scene,
   From ancient grudge break to new mutiny,
   Where civil blood makes civil hands unclean.
   From forth the fatal loins of these two foes
   A pair of star-cross'd lovers take their life;
   Whose misadventured piteous overthrows
   Do with their death bury their parents' strife.
   The fearful passage of their death-mark'd love,
   And the continuance of their parents' rage,
   Which, but their children's end, nought could remove,
   Is now the two hours' traffic of our stage; ...

I, i

Benvolio. Madam, an hour before the worshipp'd sun
 Peer'd forth the golden window of the east,
 A troubled mind drave me to walk abroad;
 Where, underneath the grove of sycamore
 That westward rooteth from the city's side,
 So early walking did I see your son:
 Towards him I made; but he was ware of me,
 And stole into the covert of the wood: . . .

Montague. Many a morning hath he there been seen,
 With tears augmenting the fresh morning's dew,
 Adding to clouds more clouds with his deep sighs:
 But all so soon as the all-cheering sun
 Should in the farthest east begin to draw
 The shady curtains from Aurora's bed,
 Away from light steals home my heavy son,
 And private in his chamber pens himself,
 Shuts up his windows, locks fair daylight out;
 And makes himself an artificial night:
 Black and portentous must this humour prove,
 Unless good counsel may the cause remove.

I, iv

Mercutio. O, then, I see Queen Mab hath been with you.
 She is the fairies' midwife, and she comes
 In shape no bigger than an agate-stone
 On the fore-finger of an alderman,
 Drawn with a team of little atomies
 Athwart men's noses as they lie asleep:
 Her waggon-spokes made of long spinners' legs;
 The cover, of the wings of grasshoppers;
 Her traces, of the smallest spider's web;
 Her collars, of the moonshine's watery beams;
 Her whip, of cricket's bone; the lash, of film;
 Her waggoner, a small grey-coated gnat,
 Not half so big as a round little worm

Prick'd from the lazy finger of a maid:
Her chariot is an empty hazel-nut,
Made by the joiner squirrel or old grub,
Time out o' mind the fairies' coachmakers.
And in this state she gallops night by night
Through lovers' brains and then they dream of love;
O'er courtiers' knees, that dream on curtsies straight;
O'er lawyers' fingers, who straight dream on fees;
O'er ladies' lips, who straight on kisses dream,
Which oft the angry Mab with blisters plagues,
Because their breaths with sweetmeats tainted are:
Sometimes she gallops o'er a courtier's nose,
Then dreams he of smelling out a suit;
And sometime comes she with a tithe-pig's tail
Tickling a parson's nose as a' lies asleep,
Then dreams he of another benefice:
Sometime she driveth o'er a soldier's neck,
And then dreams he of cutting foreign throats,
Of breaches, ambuscadoes, Spanish blades,
Of healths five fathom deep; and then anon
Drums in his ear, at which he starts and wakes,
And being thus frighted swears a prayer or two,
And sleeps again. This is that very Mab
That plats the manes of horses in the night,
And bakes the elf-locks in foul sluttish hairs
Which once untangled much misfortune bodes: . . .
                    True, I talk of dreams;
Which are the children of an idle brain,
Begot of nothing but vain fantasy,
Which is as thin of substance as the air,
And more inconstant than the wind, who wooes
Even now the frozen bosom of the north,
And, being anger'd, puffs away from thence,
Turning his face to the dew-dropping south.

I, .v

Romeo. O, she doth teach the torches to burn bright!

It seems she hangs upon the cheek of night
Like a rich jewel in an Ethiop's ear;
Beauty too rich for use, for earth too dear!
So shows a snowy dove trooping with crows,
As yonder lady o'er her fellows shows.
The measure done, I'll watch her place of stand
And, touching hers, make blessed my rude hand.
Did my heart love till now? forswear it, sight!
For I ne'er saw true beauty till this night.

II, ii

Romeo. He jests at scars that never felt a wound.
　　But, soft! what light through yonder window breaks?
　　It is the east, and Juliet is the sun!
　　Arise, fair sun, and kill the envious moon,
　　Who is already sick and pale with grief,
　　That thou her maid are far more fair than she:
　　Be not her maid, since she is envious;
　　Her vestal livery is but sick and green,
　　And none but fools do wear it; cast it off.
　　It is my lady; O, it is my love!
　　O, that she knew she were!
　　She speaks, yet she says nothing: what of that?
　　Her eye discourses, I will answer it.
　　I am too bold, 'tis not to me she speaks:
　　Two of the fairest stars in all the heaven,
　　Having some business, do intreat her eyes
　　To twinkle in their spheres till they return.
　　What if her eyes were there, they in her head?
　　The brightness of her cheek would shame those stars,
　　As daylight doth a lamp; her eyes in heaven
　　Would through the airy region stream so bright
　　That birds would sing and think it were not night.
　　See, how she leans her cheek upon her hand!
　　O, that I were a glove upon that hand,
　　That I might touch that cheek! . . .
　　　　　　　She speaks:

117

O, speak again, bright angel! for thou art
As glorious to this night, being o'er my head,
As is a winged messenger of heaven
Unto the white-upturned wondering eyes
Of mortals that fall back to gaze on him,
When he bestrides the lazy-pacing clouds
And sails upon the bosom of the air.
Juliet.   O Romeo, Romeo! wherefore art thou Romeo?
Deny thy father and refuse thy name; . . .
'Tis but thy name that is my enemy; . . .
What's in a name? that which we call a rose
By any other name would smell as sweet;
So Romeo would, were he not Romeo call'd,
Retain that dear perfection which he owes
Without that title. Romeo, doff thy name,
And for thy name, which is no part of thee,
Take all myself.
Romeo. I take thee at thy word:
Call me but love, and I'll be new baptized;
Henceforth I never will be Romeo.
Juliet. What man art thou, that, thus bescreen'd in night,
So stumbles on my counsel?
Romeo. By a name
I know not how to tell thee who I am: . . .
Juliet. How camest thou hither, tell me, and wherefore?
The orchard walls are high and hard to climb, . . .
Romeo. With love's light wings did I o'er-perch these walls,
For stony limits cannot hold love out; . . .
I have night's cloak to hide me from their eyes; . . .
Juliet. By whose direction found'st thou out this place?
Romeo. By love, that first did prompt me to inquire;
He lent me counsel, and I lent him eyes.
I am no pilot; yet, wert thou as far
As that vast shore wash'd with the farthest sea,
I would adventure for such merchandise.
Juliet. Thou know'st the mask of night is on my face,
Else would a maiden blush bepaint my cheek

For that which thou has heard me speak tonight.
Fain would I dwell on form, fain, fain deny
What I have spoke: but farewell compliment!
Dost thou love me? I know thou wilt say 'Ay,'
And I will take thy word: yet, if thou swear'st,
Thou mayst prove false; at lovers' perjuries,
They say, Jove laughs. O gentle Romeo,
If thou dost love, pronounce it faithfully:
Or if thou think'st I am too quickly won,
I'll frown and be perverse and say thee nay,
So thou wilt woo; but else, not for the world . . .
Romeo. Lady, by yonder blessed moon I swear,
That tips with silver all these fruit-tree tops, -
Juliet. O, swear not by the moon, th'inconstant moon,
That monthly changes in her circled orb,
Lest that thy love prove likewise variable . . .
                         Sweet, good night!
This bud of love, by summer's ripening breath,
May prove a beauteous flower when next we meet.
Good night, good night! as sweet repose and rest
Come to thy heart as that within my breast! . . .
My bounty is as boundless as the sea,
My love as deep; the more I give to thee,
The more I have, for both are infinite.
Juliet. Hist! Romeo, hist! - O, for a falconer's voice,
To lure this tassel-gentle back again!
Bondage is hoarse, and may not speak aloud;
Else would I tear the cave where Echo lies,
And make her airy tongue more hoarse than mine,
With repetition of my Romeo's name.
Romeo!
Romeo. It is my soul that calls upon my name:
How silver-sweet sound lovers' tongues by night,
Like softest music to attending ears! . . .
Juliet. I have forgot why I did call thee back.
Romeo. Let me stand here till thou remember it.
Juliet. I shall forget, to have thee still stand there,

Remembering how I love thy company . . .
'Tis almost morning; I would have thee gone:
And yet no farther than a wanton's bird,
Who lets it hop a little from her hand,
Like a poor prisoner in his twisted gyves,
And with a silk thread plucks it back again,
So loving-jealous of his liberty.
Romeo. I would I were thy bird.
Juliet. Sweet, so would I:
Yet I should kill thee with much cherishing.
Good night, good night! parting is such sweet sorrow
That I shall say good night till it be morrow.
Romeo. Sleep dwell upon thine eyes, peace in thy breast!
Would I were sleep and peace, so sweet to rest!

II, iii

Friar Laurence. The grey-eyed morn smiles on the frowning night,
Chequering the eastern clouds with streaks of light;
And flecked darkness like a drunkard reels
From forth day's path and Titan's fiery wheels:
Now, ere the sun advance his burning eye,
The day to cheer and night's dank dew to dry,
I must up-fill this osier cage of ours
With baleful weeds and precious-juiced flowers . . .
O, mickle is the powerful grace that lies
In herbs, plants, stones, and their true qualities:
For nought so vile that on the earth doth live,
But to the earth some special good doth give;
Nor aught so good, but, strain'd from that fair use,
Revolts from true birth, stumbling on abuse:
Virtue itself turns vice, being misapplied,
And vice sometime's by action dignified.

III, ii

Juliet. Gallop apace, you fiery-footed steeds
Towards Phoebus' lodging: such a waggoner
As Phaethon would whip you to the west,

And bring in cloudy night immediately.
Spread thy close curtain, love-performing night,
That runaways' eyes may wink, and Romeo
Leap to these arms, untalk'd of and unseen.
Lovers can see to do their amorous rites
By their own beauties; or, if love be blind,
It best agrees with night. Come, civil night,
Thou sober-suited matron, all in black,
And learn me how to lose a winning match,
Play'd for a pair of stainless maidenhoods:
Hood my unmann'd blood bating in my cheeks
With thy black mantle, till strange love grown bold
Think true love acted simple modesty.
Come, night, come, Romeo, come, thou day in night;
For thou wilt lie upon the wings of night
Whiter than new snow on a raven's back.
Come, gentle night, come, loving black-brow'd night,
Give me my Romeo; and, when he shall die,
Take him and cut him out in little stars,
And he will make the face of heaven so fine,
That all the world will be in love with night,
And pay no worship to the garish sun.
O, I have bought the mansion of a love,
But not possess'r it, and, though I am sold,
Not yet enjoy'd; so tedious is this day
As is the night before some festival
To an impatient child that hath new robes
And may not wear them.

III, v

Juliet. Wilt thou be gone? It is not yet near day:
    It was the nightingale, and not the lark,
    That pierced the fearful hollow of thine ear;
    Nightly she sings on yond pomegranate-tree:
    Believe me, love, it was the nightingale.
Romeo. It was the lark, the herald of the morn,
    No nightingale: look, love, what envious streaks

Do lace the severing clouds in yonder east:
Night's candles are burnt out, and jocund day
Stands tiptoe on the misty mountain tops:
I must be gone and live, or stay and die.

IV, .i

Juliet. O, bid me leap, rather than marry Paris,
    From off the battlements of yonder tower;
    Or walk in thievish ways; or bid me lurk
    Where serpents are; chain me with roaring bears;
    Or shut me nightly in a charnel-house,
    O'er-cover'd quite with dead men's rattling bones,
    With reeky shanks and yellow chapless skulls;
    Or bid me go into a new-made grave,
    And hide me with a dead man in his shroud;
    Things that to hear them told, have made me tremble;
    And I will do it without fear or doubt
    To live an unstain'd wife to my sweet love.

V, iii

Romeo. How oft when men are at the point of death
    Have they been merry! which their keepers call
    A lightning before death: O, how may I
    Call this a lightning? O my love! my wife!
    Death, that hath suck'd the honey of thy breath,
    Hath had no power yet upon thy beauty:
    Thou art not conquer'd; Beauty's ensign yet
    Is crimson in thy lips and in thy cheeks,
    And death's pale flag is not advanced there . . .
                Ah, dear Juliet,
    Why art thou yet so fair? shall I believe
    That unsubstantial death is amorous,
    And that the lean abhorred monster keeps
    Thee here in dark to be his paramour!
    For fear of that, I still will stay with thee,
    And never from this palace of dim night
    Depart again: here, here will I remain

With worms that are thy chamber-maids; O, here
Will I set up my everlasting rest,
And shake the yoke of inauspicious stars
From this world-wearied flesh.

JULIUS CAESAR

II, ii

Cassius. Why, man, he doth bestride the narrow world
Like a Colossus, and we petty men
Walk under his huge legs and peep about
To find ourselves dishonourable graves.
Men at some time are masters of their fates:
The fault, dear Brutus, is not in our stars,
But in ourselves, that we are underlings.

Caesar. Let me have men about me that are fat,
Sleek-headed men, and such as sleep o' nights:
Yond Cassius has a lean and hungry look;
He thinks too much: such men are dangerous; . . .
Would he were fatter! but I fear him not:

II, .i

Brutus. Boy! Lucius! Fast asleep! It is no matter;
Enjoy the honey-heavy dew of slumber:
Thou hast no figures nor no fantasies,
Which busy care draws in the brains of men;
Therefore thou sleep'st so sound.

III, i

Antony. O, pardon me, thou bleeding piece of earth,
That I am meek and gentle with these butchers!
Thou art the ruins of the noblest man
That ever lived in the tide of times.
Woe to the hand that shed this costly blood!

Over thy wounds now do I prophesy,
Which like dumb mouths do ope their ruby lips
To beg the voice and utterance of my tongue,
A curse shall light upon the limbs of men;
Domestic fury and fierce civil strife
Shall cumber all the parts of Italy;
Blood and destruction shall be so in use,
And dreadful objects so familiar,
That mothers shall but smile when they behold
Their infants quarter'd with the hands of war;
All pity choked with custom of fell deeds:
And Caesar's spirit ranging for revenge,
With Ate by his side come hot from hell,
Shall in these confines with a monarch's voice
Cry 'Havoc,'[1] and let slip the dogs of war;
That this foul deed shall smell above the earth
With carrion men, groaning for burial.

III, ii

Antony. Friends, Romans, countrymen, lend me your ears;
I come to bury Caesar, not to praise him.
The evil that men do lives after them;
The good is oft interred with their bones;
So let it be with Caesar. The noble Brutus
Hath told you Caesar was ambitious:
If it were so, it was a grievous fault,
And Grievously hath Caesar answer'd it.
Here, under leave of Brutus and the rest, -
For Brutus is an honourable man;
So are they all, all honourable men, -
Come I to speak in Caesar's funeral . . .
He hath brought many captives home to Rome,
Whose ransoms did the general coffers fill:
Did this in Caesar seem ambitious?
When that the poor have cried, Caesar hath wept:
Ambition should be made of sterner stuff:
Yet Brutus said he was ambitious;

And Brutus is an honourable man.
You all did see that on the Lupercal
I thrice presented him a kingly crown,
Which he did thrice refuse: was this ambition?
Yet Brutus says he was ambitious:
And, sure, he is an honourable man.
I speak not to disprove what Brutus spoke,
But here I am to speak what I do know.
You all did love him once, not without cause:
What cause withholds you then to mourn for him?
O judgement! thou art fled to brutish beasts,
And men have lost their reason. Bear with me;
My heart is in the coffin there with Caesar,
And I must pause till it come back to me . . .
But yesterday the world of Caesar might
Have stood against the world: now lies he there,
And none so poor to do him reverence.

Antony. If you have tears, prepare to shed them n ow.
You all do know this mantle: I remember
The first time ever Caesar put it on;
'Twas on a summer's evening, in his tent,
That day he overcame the Nervii:
Look, in this place ran Cassius' dagger through:
See what a rent the envious Casca made:
Through this the well-beloved Brutus stabb'd;
And as he pluck'd his cursed steel away,
Mark how the blood of Caesar follow'd it,
As rushing out of doors, to be resolved
If Brutus so unkindly knock'd or no:
For Brutus, as you know, was Caesar's angel:
Judge, O you gods, how dearly Caesar loved him!
This was the most unkindest cut of all;
For when the noble Caesar saw him stab,
Ingratitude, more strong than traitors' arms,
Quite vanquish'd him: then burst his mighty heart;
And, in his mantle muffling up his face,

Even at the base of Pompey's statuë,
Which all the while ran blood, great Caesar fell.
O, what a fall was there, my countrymen!
Then I, and you, and all of us fell down,
Whilst bloody treason flourish'd over us.
O, now you weep, and I perceive you feel
The dint of pity: these are gracious drops.
Kind souls, what weep you when you but behold
Our Caesar's vesture wounded? Look you here,
Here is himself, marr'd, as you see, with traitors . . .

Antony. Good friends, sweet friends, let me not stir you up
   To such a sudden flood of mutiny . . .
                    I only speak right on;
   I tell you that which you yourselves do know;
   Show you sweet Caesar's wounds, poor poor dumb mouths,
   And bid them speak for me: . . .
                    and put a tongue
   In every wound of Caesar, that should move
   The stones of Rome to rise and mutiny.

                                                            IV, iii

Brutus. There is a tide in the affairs of men
   Which taken at the flood leads on to fortune;
   Omitted, all the voyage of their life
   Is bound in shallows and in miseries.
   On such a full sea are we now afloat,
   And we must take the current when it serves,
   Or lose our ventures.
Messenger: Prepare you, generals.
   The enemy comes on in gallant show.
   Their bloody sign of battle is hung out.
   And something to be done immediately.
Anthony: Octavius, lead your battle softly on
   Upon the left hand of the even field.
Octavius: Upon the right hand, I: keep thou the left.
Anthony: Why do you cross me in this exigent?

Octavius: I do not cross you, but I will do so.

Antony. This was the noblest Roman of them all:
    All the conspirators, save only he,
    Did that they did in envy of great Caesar;
    He only, in a general honest thought
    And common good to all, made one of them.
    His life was gentle, and the elements
    So mix'd in him that Nature might stand up
    And say to all the world 'This was a man!'

HAMLET, PRINCE OF DENMARK

Marcellus. Good now, sit down, and tell me, he that knows,
    Why this same strict and most observant watch
    So nightly toils the subject of the land,
    And why such daily cast of brazen cannon,
    And foreign mart for implements of war;
    Why such impress of shipwrights, whose sore task
    Does not divide the Sunday from the week;
    What might be toward, that this sweaty haste
    Doth make the night joint-labourer with the day: . . .

    We do it wrong, being so majestical,
    To offer it the show of violence;
    For it is, as the air, invulnerable,
    And our vain blows malicious mockery.
Bernado. It was about to speak, when the cock crew.
Horatio. And then it started like a guilty thing
    Upon a fearful summons. I have heard
    The cock, that is the trumpet of the morn,
    Doth with his lofty and shrill-sounding throat
    Awake the god of day, and at his warning,

Whether in sea or fire, in earth or air,
The extravagant and erring spirit hies
To his confine: and of the truth herein
This present object made probation.
Marcellus. It faded on the crowing of the cock.
Some say that ever 'gainst that season comes
Wherein our Saviour's birth is celebrated,
The bird of dawning singeth all night long:
And then, they say, no spirit dare stir abroad,
The nights are wholesome, then no planets strike,
No fairy takes nor witch hath power to charm,
So hallow'd and so gracious is the time.
Horatio. So have I heard and do in part believe it.
But look, the morn, in russet mantle clad,
Walks o'er the dew of yon high eastward hill:
Break we our watch up;

I, ii

Hamlet. Seems, madam! nay it is; I know not 'seems.'
'Tis not alone my inky cloak, good mother,
Nor customary suits of solemn black,
Nor windy suspiration of forced breath,
No, nor the fruitful river in the eye,
Nor the dejected haviour of the visage,
Together with all forms, moods, shapes of grief,
That can denote me truly: these indeed seem,
For they are actions that a man might play:
But I have that within which passeth show;
These but the trappings and the suits of woe.
King. 'Tis sweet and commendable in your nature, Hamlet,
To give these mourning duties to your father:
But, you must know, your father lost a father,
That father lost, lost his, and the survivor bound
In filial obligation for some term
To do obsequious sorrow: but to persever
In obstinate condolement is a course
Of impious stubbornness; 'tis unmanly grief:

128

Shakespeare

It shows a will most incorrect to heaven,
A heart unfortified, a mind impatient,
An understanding simple and unschool'd:
For what we know must be and is as common
As any the most vulgar thing to sense,
Why should we in our peevish opposition
Take it to heart?

Hamlet: O, that this too too solid flesh would melt,
Thaw and resolve itself into a dew!
Or that the Everlasting had not fix'd
His canon 'gainst self-slaughter! O God! God!
How weary, stale, flat and unprofitable
Seem to me all the uses of this world!
Fie on't! ah fie! 'tis an unweeded garden,
That grows to seed; . . .
                    That it should come to this! . . .
So excellent a king; that was, to this,
Hyperion to a satyr: so loving to my mother,
That he might not beteem the winds of heaven
Visit her face too roughly. Heaven and earth!
Must I remember? why, she would hang on him,
As if increase of appetite had grown
By what it fed on: . . .
                    - Frailty, thy name is woman! -
A little month, or ere those shoes were old
With which she follow'd my poor father's body,
Like Niobe, all tears: . . .
                    - married with my uncle,
My father's brother, but no more like my father
Than I to Hercules: within a month;
Ere yet the salt of most unrighteous tears
Had left the flushing in her galled eyes,
She married . . .
It is not, nor it cannot come to good:
But break, my heart, for I must hold my tongue!

Polonius. Yet here, Laertes! . . .
            There; my blessing with thee
And these few precepts in thy memory
Look thou character. Give thy thoughts no tongue,
Nor any unproportion'd thought his act.
Be thou familiar, but by no means vulgar.
Those friends thou hast, and their adoption tried,
Grapple them to thy soul with hoops of steel,
But do not dull thy palm with entertainment
Of each new-hatch'd unfledged comrade. Beware
Of entrance to a quarrel: but being in,
Bear't, that the opposed may beware of thee.
Give every man thy ear, but few thy voice:
Take each man's censure, but reserve thy judgement.
Costly thy habit as thy purse can buy,
But not express'd in fancy; rich, not gaudy:
For the apparel oft proclaims the man;
And they in France of the best rank and station
Are of a most select and generous chief in that.
Neither a borrower nor a lender be:
For loan oft loses both itself and friend,
And borrowing dulls the edge of husbandry.
This above all: to thine own self be true,
And it must follow, as the night the day,
Thou canst not then be false to any man.[3]

Hamlet. The king doth wake to-night and takes his rouse,
    Keeps wassail, and the swaggering up-spring reels;
    And as he drains his draughts of Rhenish down,
    The kettle-drum and trumpets thus bray out
    The triumph of his pledge.
Horatio. Is it a custom?
Hamlet. Ay, marry, is't:
    But to my mind, though I am native here
    And to the manner born, it is a custom

Shakespeare

More honour'd in the breach than the observance.

I, v

Ghost. I am thy father's spirit;
    Doom'd for a certain term to walk the night,
    And for the day confined to fast in fires,
    Till the foul crimes done in my days of nature
    Are burnt and purged away. But that I am forbid
    To tell the secrets of my prison-house,
    I could a tale unfold whose lightest word
    Would harrow up thy soul, freeze thy young blood,
    Make thy two eyes, like stars, start from their spheres,
    Thy knotted and combined locks to part
    And each particular hair to stand on end,
    Like quills upon the fretful porpentine:
    But this eternal blazon must not be
    To ears of flesh and blood . . .

II, ii

Hamlet. I will tell you why; . . . I have of late . . . lost all my mirth, forgone all custom of exercises; and indeed it goes so heavily with my disposition that this goodly frame, the earth, seems to me a sterile promontory; this most excellent canopy, the air, look you, this brave o'erhanging firmament, this majestical roof fretted with golden fire, why, it appears no other thing to me than a foul and pestilent congregation of vapours. What a piece of work is a man! how noble in reason! how infinite in faculty! in form and moving how express and admirable! in action how like an angel! in apprehension how like a god! the beauty of the world! the paragon of animals! . . .

Hamlet. O, what a rogue and peasant slave am I!
    Is it not monstrous that this player here,
    But in a fiction, in a dream of passion,
    Could force his soul so to his own conceit
    That from her working all his visage wann'd;
    Tears in his eyes, distraction in's aspect,
    A broken voice, and his whole function suiting
    With forms to his conceit? and all for nothing!

For Hecuba!
What's Hecuba to him, or he to Hecuba,
That he should weep for her? What would he do,
Had he the motive and the cue for passion
That I have? He would drown the stage with tears
And cleave the general ear with horrid speech,
Make mad the guilty and appal the free,
Confound the ignorant, and amaze indeed
The very faculties of eyes and ears.
Yet I,
A dull and muddy-mettled rascal, peak,
Like John-a-dreams, unpregnant of my cause . . .
Why, what an ass am I! This is most brave,
That I, the son of a dear father murder'd,
Prompted to my revenge by heaven and hell,
Must, like a whore, unpack my heart with words,
And fall a-cursing, like a very drab, . . .
                              The play's the thing
Wherein I'll catch the conscience of the king.

                                                        III, i

Hamlet. To be, or not to be: that is the question:
    Whether 'tis nobler in the mind to suffer
    The slings and arrows of outrageous fortune,
    Or to take arms against a sea of troubles,
    And by opposing end them. To die: to sleep;
    No more; and by a sleep to say we end
    The heart-ache, and the thousand natural shocks
    That flesh is heir to, 'tis a consummation
    Devoutly to be wish'd. To die, to sleep;
    To sleep: perchance to dream: ay, there's the rub;
    For in that sleep of death what dreams may come,
    When we have shuffled off this mortal coil,
    Must give us pause: there's the respect
    That makes calamity of so long life;
    For who would bear the whips and scorns of time.
    The oppressor's wrong, the proud man's contumely,

The pangs of despised love, the law's delay,
The insolence of office, and the spurns
That patient merit of the unworthy takes,
When he himself might his quietus make
With a bare bodkin? who would fardels bear,
To grunt and sweat under a weary life,
But that the dread of something after death,
The undiscover'd country from whose bourn
No traveller returns, puzzles the will,
And make us rather bear those ills we have
Than fly to others that we know not of?
Thus conscience does make cowards of us all,
And thus the native hue of resolution
Is sicklied o'er with the pale cast of thought,
And enterprises of great pitch and moment
With this regard their currents turn awry
And lose the name of action . . .

Ophelia. O, what a noble mind is here o'erthrown!
The courtier's, soldier's, scholar's, eye, tongue, sword:
The expectancy and rose of the fair state,
The glass of fashion and the mould of form,
The observed of all observers, quite, quite down!
And I, of ladies most deject and wretched,
That suck'd the honey of his music vows,
Now see that noble and most sovereign reason,
Like sweet bells jangled, out of tune and harsh;
That unmatch'd form and feature of blown youth
Blasted with ecstasy: O, woe is me, . . .

III, ii

Hamlet.
Speak the speech, I pray you, as I pronounced it to you, trippingly on the
tongue: but if you mouth it, as many of your players do, I had as lief the town-
crier spoke my lines. Nor do not saw the air too much with your hand, thus;
but use all gently: for in the very torrent, tempest, and, as I may say, whirlwind
of your passion, you must acquire and beget a temperance that may give it

smoothness. O, it offends me to the soul to hear a robustious periwig-pated fellow tear a passion to tatters, to very rags, to split the ears of the groundlings, who, for the most part, are capable of nothing but inexplicable dumb-shows and noise: I would have such a fellow whipped for o'erdoing Termagant; it out-herods Herod: pray you, avoid it . . .
Be not too tame neither, but let your own discretion be your tutor: suit the action to the word, the word to the action; with this special observance, that you o'erstep not the modesty of nature: for anything so overdone is from the purpose of playing, whose end, both at the first and now, was and is, to hold, as 'twere the mirror up to nature; to show virtue her own feature, scorn her own image, and the very age and body of the time his form and pressure. Now this overdone or come tardy off, though it make the unskilful laugh, cannot but make the judicious grieve; the censure of the which one must in your allowance o'erweigh a whole theatre of others.[4]

Hamlet.   Nay, do not think I flatter; . . .
          Why should the poor be flatter'd?
No, let the candied tongue lick absurd pomp,
And crook the pregnant hinges of the knee
Where thrift may follow fawning . . .
                    Give me that man
That is not passion's slave, and I will wear him
In my heart's core, ay, in my heart of heart,
As I do thee . . .
Player King. Full thirty times hath Phoebus' cart gone round
    Neptune's salt wash and Tellus' orbed ground,
    And thirty dozen moons with borrowed sheen
    About the world have times twelve thirties been,
    Since love our hearts and Hymen did our hands
    Unite commutual in most sacred bands.
Player Queen. So many journeys may the sun and moon
    Make us again count o'er ere love be done!

Hamlet. 'Tis now the very witching time of night,
    When churchyards yawn, and hell itself breathes out
    Contagion to this world: now could I drink hot blood,
    And do such bitter business as the day

Would quake to look on . . .

III, iii

Rosencrantz. The single and peculiar life is bound
   With all the strength and armour of the mind
   To keep itself from noyance; but much more
   That spirit upon whose weal depends and rests
   The lives of many. The cease of majesty
   Dies not alone, but like a gulf doth draw
   What's near it with it: it is a massy wheel,
   Fix'd on the summit of the highest mount,
   To whose huge spokes ten thousand lesser things
   Are mortised and adjoin'd; which, when it falls,
   Each small annexment, petty consequence,
   Attends the boisterous ruin. Never alone
   Did the king sigh, but with a general groan . . .

III, iv

Hamlet. Look here, upon this picture, and on this, . . .
   See what a grace was seated on this brow;
   Hyperion's curls, the front of Jove himself,
   An eye like Mars, to threaten and command;
   A station like the herald Mercury
   New-lighted on a heaven-kissing hill;
   A combination and a form indeed,
   Where every god did seem to set his seal
   To give the world assurance of a man:
   This was your husband.

IV, iv

Hamlet. How all occasions do inform against me,
   And spur my dull revenge! What is a man,
   If his chief good and market of his time
   Be but to sleep and feed? a beast, no more.
   Sure, he that made us with such large discourse,
   Looking before and after, gave us not
   That capability and god-like reason

To fust in us unused. Now, whether it be
Bestial oblivion, or some craven scruple
Of thinking too precisely on the event, -
A thought which, quarter'd, hath but one part wisdom
And ever three parts coward, - I do not know
Why yet I live to say 'this thing's to do,'
Sith I have cause, and will, and strength, and means,
To do't. Examples gross as earth exhort me:
Witness this army, of such mass and charge,
Led by a delicate and tender prince,
Whose spirit with divine ambition puff'd
Makes mouths at the invisible event,
Exposing what is mortal and unsure
To all that fortune, death and danger dare,
Even for an egg-shell. Rightly to be great
Is not to stir without great argument,
But greatly to find quarrel in a straw
When honour's at the stake. How stand I then,
That have a father kill'd, a mother stain'd,
Excitements of my reason and my blood,
And let all sleep, while to my shame I see
The imminent death of twenty thousand men,
That for a fantasy and trick of fame
Go to their graves like beds, fight for a plot
Whereon the numbers cannot try the cause,
Which is not tomb enough and continent
To hide the slain? O, from this time forth,
My thoughts be bloody, or be nothing worth!

IV, vii

Queen. One woe doth tread upon another's heel,
    So fast they follow: your sister's drown'd, Laertes, . . .
    There is a willow grows aslant a brook,
    That shows his hoar leaves in the glassy stream;
    There with fantastic garlands did she come
    Of crow-flowers, nettles, daisies and long purples,
    That liberal shepherds give a grosser name,

But our cold maids do dead men's fingers call them:
There, on the pendent boughs her coronet weeds
Clambering to hang, an envious sliver broke;
When down her weedy trophies and herself
Fell in the weeping brook. Her clothes spread wide,
And mermaid-like a while they bore her up:
Which times she chanted snatches of old tunes,
As one incapable of her own distress,
Or like a creature native and indued
Unto that element: but long it could not be
Till that her garments, heavy with their drink,
Pull'd the poor wretch from her melodious lay
To muddy death.

V, i

Hamlet:
Alas, poor Yorick. I knew him, Horatio - a fellow of infinite jest, of most excellent fancy. He hath borne me on his back a thousand times; and now, how abhorred my imagination is! My gorge rises at it. Here hung those lips that I have kissed I know not how oft. Where be your gibes now, your gambols, your songs, your flashes of merriment that were wont to set the table on a roar? Not one now to mock your own grinning? Quite chop-fallen? Now get you back to my lady's chamber and tell her, let her paint an inch thick, to this favour she must come. Make her laugh at that.[5]

V, ii

Hamlet. Our indiscretion sometime serves us well
When our deep plots do pall; and that should learn us
There's a divinity that shapes our ends,
Rough-hew them how we will.

V, ii

Hamlet. O good Horatio, what a wounded name,
Things standing thus unknown, shall live behind me!
If thou didst ever hold me in thy heart,
Absent thee from felicity a while,
And in this harsh world draw thy breath in pain,

137

To tell my story . . .
The rest is silence.

OTHELLO

Othello. Most potent, grave, and reverend signiors,
My very noble and approved good masters,
That I have ta'en away this old man's daughter,
It is most true; true, I have married her:
The very head and front of my offending
Hath this extent, no more. Rude am I in my speech,
And little blest with the soft phrase of peace;
For since these arms of mine had seven years' pith,
Till now some nine moons wasted, they have used
Their dearest action in the tented field;
And little of this great world can I speak,
More than pertains to feats of broil and battle;
And therefore little shall I grace my cause
In speaking for myself. Yet, by your gracious patience,
I will a round unvarnish'd tale deliver
Of my whole course of love; what drugs, what charms,
What conjuration and what mighty magic -
For such proceeding I am charged withal -
I won his daughter.
Brabantio. A maiden never bold;
Of spirit so still and quiet that her motion
Blush'd at herself; and she - in spite of nature,
Of years, of country, credit, every thing -
To fall in love with what she fear'd to look on! . . .

Othello. Her father loved me, oft invited me,
Still questioned me the story of my life
From year to year, the battles, sieges, fortunes
That I have pass'd.

Shakespeare

I ran it through, even from my boyish days
To the very moment that he bade me tell it
Wherein I spake of most disastrous chances,
Of moving accidents by flood and field,
Of hair-breadth 'scapes i' the imminent deadly breach,
Of being taken by the insolent foe,
And sold to slavery, of my redemption thence,
And portance in my travels' history:
Wherein of antres[6] vast and deserts idle,
Rough quarries, rocks, and hills whose heads touch heaven,
It was my hint to speak, - such was the process;
And of the Cannibals that each other eat,
The Anthropophagi,[7] and men whose heads
Do grow beneath their shoulders. This to hear
Would Desdemona seriously incline:
But still the house-affairs would draw her thence:
Which ever as she could with haste dispatch,
She'ld come again, and with a greedy ear
Devour up my discourse: which I observing,
Took once a pliant hour, and found good means
To draw from her a prayer of earnest heart
That I would all my pilgrimage dilate,
Whereof by parcels she had something heard,
But not intentively: I did consent,
And often did beguile her of her tears
When I did speak of some distressful stroke
That my youth suffer'd. My story being done,
She gave me for my pains a world of sighs:
She swore, in faith, 'twas strange, 'twas passing strange;
'Twas pitiful, 'twas wondrous pitiful:
She wish'd she had not heard it, yet she wish'd
That heaven had made her such a man: she thank'd me,
And bade me, if I had a friend that loved her,
I should but teach him how to tell my story,
And that would woo her. Upon this hint I spake:
She loved me for the dangers I had pass'd,
And I loved her that she did pity them.

This only is the witchcraft I have used.

III, iii

Iago. Good name in man and woman, dear my lord,
    Is the immediate jewel of their souls;
    Who steals my purse steals trash; 'tis something, nothing;
    'Twas mine, 'tis his, and has been slave to thousands;
    But he that filches from me my good name
    Robs me of that which not enriches him
    And makes me poor indeed.
Iago. Trifles light as air
    Are to the jealous confirmations strong
    As proofs of holy writ: . . .
    Dangerous conceits are in their natures poisons:
    Which at the first are scarce found to distaste,
    But with a little act upon the blood
    Burn like the mines of sulphur . . .

Othello. Avaunt! be gone! thou hast set me on the rack:
    I swear 'tis better to be much abused
    Than but to know't a little . . .
                    O, now for ever
    Farewell the tranquil mind! farewell content!
    Farewell the plumed troop and the big wars
    That make ambition virtue! O, farewell,
    Farewell the neighing steed and the shrill trump,
    The spirit-stirring drum, the ear-piercing fife,
    The royal banner and all quality,
    Pride, pomp and circumstance of glorious war!
    And, O you mortal engines, whose rude throats
    The immortal Jove's dread clamours counterfeit,
    Farewell! Othello's occupation's gone!

V, ii

Othello. It is the cause, it is the cause, my soul:
    Let me not name it to you, you chaste stars!
    It is the cause. Yet I'll not shed her blood

Nor scar that whiter skin of hers than snow
And smooth as monumental alabaster.
Yet she must die, else she'll betray more men
Put out the light, and then put out the light:
If I quench thee, thou flaming minister,
I can again thy former light restore,
Should I repent me: but once put out thy light
Thou cunning'st pattern of excelling nature,
I know not where is that Promethean heat
That can thy light relume. When I have pluck'd the rose,
I cannot give it vital growth again,
It must needs wither; I'll smell it on the tree.
Ah, balmy breath, thou dost almost persuade
Justice to break her sword! One more, one more:
Be thus when thou art dead, and I will kill thee,
And love thee after: once more, and this the last:
So sweet was ne'er so fatal. I must weep,
But they are cruel tears: this sorrow's heavenly;
It strikes where it doth love.

Othello. Soft you; a word or two before you go . . .
                    I pray you, in your letters,
When you shall these unlucky deeds relate,
Speak of me as I am; nothing extenuate,
Nor set down aught in malice: then must you speak
Of one that loved not wisely but too well;
Of one not easily jealous, but, being wrought,
Perplex'd in the extreme; of one whose hand,
Like the base Indian, threw a pearl away
Richer than all his tribe; of one whose subdued eyes,
Albeit unused to the melting mood,
Drop tears as fast as the Arabian trees
Their medicinal gum.

KING LEAR

France. This is most strange,
  That she, that even but now was your best object,
  The argument of your praise, balm of your age,
  Most best, most dearest, should in this trice of time
  Commit a thing so monstrous, to dismantle
  So many folds of favour . . .

Cordelia. I yet beseech your majesty, -
  If for I want that glib and oily art, . . .
  It is no vicious blot, murder, or foulness,
  No unchaste action, or dishonour'd step,
  That hath deprived me of your grace and favour; . . .

France. Fairest Cordelia, that art most rich being poor,
  Most choice forsaken, and most loved despised,
  Thee and thy virtues here I seize upon:
  Be it lawful I take up what's cast away
  Gods, gods! 'tis strange that from their cold'st neglect
  My love should kindle to inflamed respect.
  Thy dowerless daughter, king, thrown to my chance,
  Is queen of us, of ours, and our fair France:

Kent. I do profess to be no less than I seem; to serve him truly that will put me
  in trust; to love him that is honest; to converse with him that is wise and says
  little; to fear judgement; to fight when I cannot choose, and to eat no fish.*
  . . .

  * (i.e. remain a Protestant - Roman Catholics ate fish on Fridays).

Lear. It may be so, my lord,
  Hear, nature, hear; dear Goddess, hear!
  Suspend thy purpose, if thou didst intent
  To make this creature fruitful:
  Into her womb convey sterility:
  Dry up in her the organs of increase,

And from her derogate body never spring
A babe to honour her! If she must teem,
Create her child of spleen, . . .
              that she may feel
How sharper than a serpent's tooth it is
To have a thankless child! . . .
              Life and death! I am ashamed
That thou hast power to shake my manhood thus;
That these hot tears, which break from me perforce,
Should make these worth them.

II, iv

Lear. O, reason not the need: our basest beggars
   Are in the poorest thing superfluous:
   Allow not nature more than nature needs,
   Man's life's as cheap as beast's: . . .
              But for true need, -
   You heavens, give me that patience, patience I need!
   You see me here, you gods, a poor old man,
   As full of grief as age; wretched in both:
   If it be you that stirs these daughters' hearts
   Against their father, fool me not so much
   To bear it tamely; touch me with noble anger,
   And let not woman's weapons, water-drops,
   Stain my man's cheeks!

III, i

Kent. Where's the king?
Gentleman. Contending with the fretful elements;
   Bids the wind blow the earth into the sea,
   Or swell the curled waters 'bove the main,
   That things might change or cease; tears his white hair,
   Which the impetuous blasts, with eyeless rage,
   Catch in their fury, and make nothing of;
   Strives in his little world of man to out-scorn
   The to-and-fro-conflicting wind and rain.
   This night, wherein the cub-drawn bear would couch,
   The lion and the belly-pinched wolf

143

Keep their fur dry, unbonneted he runs,
And bids what will take all.

III, ii

Lear. Blow, winds, and crack your cheeks! rage! blow!
    You cataracts and hurricanoes, spout
    Till you have drench'd our steeples, drown'd the cocks!
    You sulphurous and thought-executing fires,
    Vaunt-couriers to oak-cleaving thunderbolts,
    Singe my white head! And thou, all-shaking thunder,
    Smite flat the thick rotundity o' the world!
    Crack nature's moulds, all germins spill at once
    That make ingrateful man! . . .

Lear. Rumble thy bellyful! Spit, fire! spout, rain.
    Nor rain, wind, thunder, fire, are my daughters:
    I tax not you, you elements, with unkindness;
    I never gave you kingdom, call'd you children,
    You owe me no subscription: then let fall
    Your horrible pleasure; here I stand, your slave,
    A poor, infirm, weak and despised old man;
    But yet I call you servile ministers,
    That have with two pernicious daughters join'd
    Your high-engender'd battles 'gainst a head
    So old and white as this. O! O! 'tis foul!
Kent. Alas, sir, are you here? things that love night
    Love not such nights as these; the wrathful skies
    Gallow the very wanderers of the dark,
    And make them keep their caves; since I was man
    Such sheets of fire, such bursts of horrid thunder,
    Such groans of roaring wind and rain, I never
    Remember to have heard: man's nature cannot carry
    The affliction nor the fear.

III, iv

Lear. Prithee, go in thyself; seek thine own ease: . . .
    Poor naked wretches, whereso'er you are,

That bide the pelting of this pitiless storm,
How shall your houseless heads and unfed sides,
Your loop'd and window'd raggedness, defend you
From seasons such as these? O, I have ta'en
Too little care of this! Take physic, pomp;
Expose thyself to feel what wretches feel,
That thou mayst shake the superflux to them
And show the heavens more just.

IV, iii

Gentleman. Ay, sir; she took them, read them in my presence
And now and then an ample tear trill'd down
Her delicate cheek: it seem'd she was a queen
Over her passion, who most rebel-like
Sought to be king o'er her.
Kent. O, then it moved her.
Gentleman. Not to a rage: patience and sorrow strove
Who should express her goodliest. You have seen
Sunshine and rain at once: her smiles and tears
Were like a better way: those happy smilets
That play'd on her ripe lip seem'd not to know
What guests were in her eyes; which parted thence
As pearls from diamonds dropp'd. In brief,
Sorrow would be a rarity most beloved,
If all could so become it.

IV,vi

Edgar. Come on, sir; here's the place: stand still. How fearful
And dizzy 'tis to cast one's eyes so low!
The crows and choughs that wing the midway air
Show scarce so gross as beetles: half way down
Hangs one that gathers samphire, dreadful trade!
Methink he seems no bigger than his head:
The fishermen that walk upon the beach
Appear like mice; and yond tall anchoring bark
Diminish'd to her cock; her cock, a buoy
Almost too small for sight: the murmuring surge
That on the unnumbere'd idle pebbles chafes

Cannot be heard so high. I'll look no more,
Lest my brain turn and the deficient sight
Topple down headlong.

Lear. No, no, no, no! Come, let's away to prison:
We two alone will sing like birds i' the cage:
When thou dost ask me blessing, I'll kneel down
And ask of thee forgiveness: so we'll live,
And pray, and sing, and tell old tales, and laugh
At gilded butterflies, and hear poor rogues
Talk of court news; and we'll talk with them too,
Who loses and who wins, who's in, who's out;
And take upon's the mystery of things,
As if we were God's spies: and we'll wear out,
In a wall'd prison, packs and sects of great ones
That ebb and flow by the moon.

MACBETH

Lady Macbeth. The raven himself is hoarse
That croaks the fatal entrance of Duncan
Under my battlements. Come, you spirits
That tend on mortal thoughts, unsex me here,
And fill me, from the crown to the toe, top-full
Of direst cruelty! make thick my blood,
Stop up the access and passage to remorse,
That no compunctious visitings of nature
Shake my fell purpose, nor keep peace between
The effect and it! Come to my woman's breasts,
And take my milk for gall, you murdering ministers,
Wherever in your sightless substances
You wait on nature's mischief! Come, thick night,
And pall thee in the dunnest smoke of hell,

That my keen knife see not the wound it makes,
Nor heaven peep through the blanket of the dark,
To cry 'Hold, hold!'

I, vi

Duncan. This castle hath a pleasant seat; the air
    Nimbly and sweetly recommends itself
    Unto our gentle senses.
Banquo. This guest of summer,
    The temple-haunting martlet, does approve
    By his loved mansionry that the heavens' breath
    Smells wooingly here: no jutty, frieze,
    Buttress, nor coign of vantage, but this bird
    Hath made his pendant bed and procreant cradle:
    Where they most breed and haunt, I have observed
    The air is delicate.

I, vii

Macbeth. If it were done when 'tis done, then 'twere well
    It were done quickly: if the assassination
    Could trammel up the consequence, and catch,
    With his surcease, success; that but this blow
    Might be the be-all and the end-all here,
    But here, upon this bank and shoal of time,
    We'ld jump the life to come. But in these cases
    We still have judgement here; that we but teach
    Bloody instructions, which being taught return
    To plague the inventor: this even-handed justice
    Commends the ingredients of our poison'd chalice
    To our own lips. He's here in double trust:
    First, as I am his kinsman and his subject,
    Strong both against the deed; then as his host,
    Who should against his murderer shut the door,
    Not bear the knife myself. Besides, this Duncan
    Hath borne his faculties so meek, hath been
    So clear in his great office, that his virtues
    Will plead like angels trumpet-tongued against

The deep damnation of his taking-off;
And pity, like a naked, new-born babe,
Striding the blast, or heaven's cherubim horsed
Upon the sightless couriers of the air,
Shall blow the horrid deed in every eye,
That tears shall drown the wind. I have no spur
To prick the sides of my intent, but only
Vaulting ambition, which o'erleaps itself
And falls on the other.

II, i

Macbeth. Is this a dagger which I see before me,
The handle toward my hand? Come, let me clutch thee.
I have thee not, and yet I see thee still.
Art thou not, fatal vision, sensible
To feeling as to sight? or art thou but
A dagger of the mind, a false creation,
Proceeding from the heat-oppressed brain?
I see thee yet, in form as palpable
As this which now I draw . . .
                              I see thee still;
And on thy blade and dudgeon gouts of blood,
Which was not so before. There's no such thing:
It is the bloody business which informs
Thus to mine eyes. Now o'er the one half-world
Nature seems dead, and wicked dreams abuse
The curtain'd sleep; witchcraft celebrates
Pale Hecate's offerings; and wither'd murder,
Alarum'd by his sentinel, the wolf,
Whose howl's his watch, thus with his stealthy pace,
With Tarquin's ravishing strides, towards his design
Moves like a ghost. Thou sure and firm-set earth,
Hear not my steps, which way they walk, for fear
Thy very stones prate of my whereabout,
And take the present horror from the time,
Which now suits with it.

Macbeth. Methought I heard a voice cry 'Sleep no more!
  Macbeth does murder sleep' - the innocent sleep,
  Sleep that knits up the ravell'd sleave of care,
  The death of each day's life, sore labour's bath,
  Balm of hurt minds, great nature's second course,
  Chief nourisher in life's feast, -
Lady Macbeth. What do you mean?
Macbeth. Still it cried 'Sleep no more!' to all the house:
  'Glamis hath murder'd sleep, and therefore Cawdor
  Shall sleep no more: Macbeth shall sleep no more.'

Macbeth. Whence is that knocking?
  How is't with me, when every noise appals me?
  What hands are here? ha! they pluck out mine eyes!
  Will all great Neptune's ocean wash this blood
  Clean from my hand? No; this my hand will rather
  The multitudinous seas incarnadine,
  Making the green one red.

Macbeth. Then be thou jocund: ere the bat hath flown
  His cloister'd flight; ere to black Hecate's summons
  The shard-borne beetle with his drowsy hums
  Hath rung night's yawning peal, there shall be done
  A deed of dreadful note . . .
                  Come, seeling night,
  Scarf up the tender eye of pitiful day,
  And with thy bloody and invisible hand
  Cancel and tear to pieces that great bond
  Which keeps me pale! Light thickens, and the crow
  Makes wing to the rooky wood:
  Good things of day begin to droop and drowse,
  Whiles night's black agents to their preys do rouse.

First Murderer. The west yet glimmers with some streaks of day:

Now spurs the lated traveller apace
To gain the timely inn.

Macbeth. Tomorrow, and tomorrow, and tomorrow,
   Creeps in this petty pace from day to day,
   To the last syllable of recorded time;
   And all our yesterdays have lighted fools
   The way to dusty death. Out, out, brief candle!
   Life's but a walking shadow, a poor player
   That struts and frets his hour upon the stage
   And then is heard no more: it is a tale
   Told by an idiot, full of sound and fury,
   Signifying nothing.

ANTONY AND CLEOPATRA

Agrippa. To hold you in perpetual amity,
   To make you brothers and to knit your hearts
   With an unslipping knot, take Antony
   Octavia to his wife; whose beauty claims
   No worse a husband than the best of men,
   Whose virtue and whose general graces speak
   That which none else can utter. By this marriage,
   All little jealousies which now seem great,
   And all great fears which now import their dangers,
   Would then be nothing:

Enobarbus. The barge she sat in, like a burnish'd throne,
   Burn'd on the water: the poop was beaten gold;
   Purple the sails, and so perfumed that
   The winds were love-sick with them; the oars were silver,
   Which to the tune of flutes kept stroke and made
   The water which they beat to follow faster,

As amorous of their strokes. For her own person,
It beggar'd all description: she did lie
In her pavilion, cloth-of-gold of tissue.
O'er picturing that Venus, where we see
The fancy out-work nature: on each side her
Stood pretty dimpled boys, like smiling Cupids,
With divers-colour'd fans, whose wind did seem
To glow the delicate cheeks which they did cool,
And what they undid did.
Agrippa. O, rare for Antony!
Enobarbus. Her gentlewomen, like the Nereides,
So many mermaids, tended her i' the eyes,
And made their bends adornings: at the helm
A seeming mermaid steers: the silken tackle
Swell with the touches of those flower-soft hands,
That yarely frame the office. From the barge
A strange invisible perfume hits the sense
Of the adjacent wharfs. The city cast
Her people out upon her; and Antony,
Enthroned i' the market-place, did sit alone,
Whistling to the air; which, but for vacancy,
Had gone to gaze on Cleopatra too,
And made a gap in nature.
Agrippa. Rare Egyptian!

Enobarbus.

. . .

Age cannot wither her, nor custom stale
Her infinite variety: other women cloy
The appetites they feed, but she makes hungry
Where most she satisfies: for vilest things
Become themselves in her, that the holy priests
Bless her when she is riggish.

Part IV

CORIOLANUS

IIII, ii

Volumnia. Because that now it lies you on to speak
  To the people; not by your own instruction,
  Nor by the matter which your heart prompts you,
  But with such words that are but roted in
  Your tongue, though but bastards and syllables
  Of no allowance, to your bosom's truth.
  Now, this no more dishonours you at all,
  Than to take in a town with gentle words,
  Which else would put you to your fortune and
  The hazard of much blood.

Coriolanus. Away, my disposition, and possess me
  Some harlot's spirit! my throat of war be turn'd,
  Which quired with my drum, into a pipe
  Small as a eunuch, or the virgin voice
  That babies lulls asleep! the smiles of knaves
  Tent in my cheek, and schoolboys' tears take up
  The glasses of my sight! a beggar's tongue
  Make motion through my lips, and my arm'd knees,
  Who bow'd but in my stirrup, bend like his
  That hath received an alms! I will not do't;
  Lest I surcease to honour mine own truth,
  And by my body's action teach my mind
  A most inherent baseness.

V, iii

Volumnia. Nay, go not from us thus . . .
               Thou know'st, great son,
  The end of war's uncertain: but this certain,
  That, if thou conquer Rome, the benefit
  Which thou shalt thereby reap is such a name
  Whose repetition will be dogg'd with curses; . . .
  Thou hast affected the fine strains of honour,
  To imitate the graces of the gods;
  To tear with thunder the wide cheeks o' the air

And yet to charge thy sulphur with a bolt
That should but rive an oak . . .
                    Thou hast never in thy life
Show'd thy dear mother any courtesy;
When she, poor hen, fond of no second brood,
Has cluck'd thee to the wars, and safely home,
Loaden with honour. Say my request's unjust,
And spurn me back; but if it be not so,
Thou art not honest, and the gods will plague thee,
That thou restrain'st from me the duty which
To a mother's part belongs.

PERICLES, PRINCE OF TYRE

III, ii

Cerimon. I hold it ever,
    Virtue and cunning were endowments greater
    Than nobleness and riches: careless heirs
    May the two latter darken and expend,
    But immortality attends the former,
    Making a man a god . . .

Cerimon. For look how fresh she looks! They were too rough
    That threw her in the sea. Make a fire within:
    Fetch hither all my boxes in my closet,
    Death may usurp on nature many hours,
    And yet the fire of life kindle again
    The o'erpress'd spirits . . .
    Well said, well said; the fire and cloths.
    The rough and woful music that we have,
    Cause it to sound, beseech you.
    The viol once more: how thou stirr'st, thou block!
    The music there! I pray you give her air . . .

Cerimon. She is alive; behold,

Her eyelids, cases to those heavenly jewels
Which Pericles has lost, begin to part
Their fringes of bright gold: the diamonds
Of a most praised water do appear
To make the world twice rich.

CYMBELINE

II, ii

Iachimo. The crickets sing, and man's o'er-labour'd sense
    Repairs itself by rest. Our Tarquin thus
    Did softly press the rushes, ere he waken'd
    The chastity he wounded. Cytherea,
    How bravely thou becomest thy bed! fresh lily!
    And whiter than the sheets! That I might touch
    But kiss; one kiss! Rubies unparagon'd,
    How dearly they do't! 'Tis her breathing that
    Perfumes the chamber thus: the flame o' the taper
    Bows toward her, and would under-peep her lids
    To see the unclosed lights, now canopied
    Under those windows, white and azure, lac'd
    With blue of heaven's own tinct . . .
    O sleep, thou ape of death, lie dull upon her!
    And be her sense but as a monument,
    Thus in a chapel lying!

III, ii

Belarius. Now for our mountain sport. Up to yond hill!
    Your legs are young: I'll tread these flat. Consider,
    When you above perceive me like a crow,
    That it is place which lessens and sets off:
    And you may then revolve what tales I have told you
    Of courts, of princes, of the tricks in war: . . .
    And often, to our comfort, shall we find

The sharded beetle in a safer hold
Than is the full-wing'd eagle. O, this life
Is nobler than attending for a check,
Richer than doing nothing for a bauble,
Prouder than rustling in unpaid-for silk:

IV, ii

Guiderius	Fear no more the heat o' the sun,
	Nor the furious winter's rages;
	Thou thy worldly task hast done,
	Home art gone and ta'en thy wages:
	Golden lads and girls all must,
	As chimney-sweepers, come to dust.
Arviragus	Fear no more the frown o' the great;
	Thou art past the tyrant's stroke;
	Care no more to clothe and eat;
	To thee the reed is as the oak:
	The sceptre, learning, physic, must
	All follow this and come to dust.
Guiderius	Fear no more the lightning flash,
	Nor the all-dreaded thunder-stone;
and	Fear not slander, censure rash;
	Thou hast finish'd joy and moan:
Arviragus	All lovers young, all lovers must
	Consign to thee and come to dust.
Guiderius	No exorciser harm thee!
	Nor no witchcraft charm thee!
and	Ghost unlaid forbear thee!
	Nothing ill come near thee!
Arviragus	Quiet consummation have;
	And renowned be thy grave![6]

V, v

Soothsayer. The fingers of the powers above do tune

The harmony of peace. The vision,
Which I made known to Lucius ere the stroke
Of this yet scarce-cold battle, at this instant
Is full accomplish'd; for the Roman eagle,
From south to west on wing soaring aloft,
Lessen'd herself and in the beams o' the sun
So vanish'd: which foreshow'd our princely eagle,
The imperial Caesar, should again unite
His favour with the radiant Cymbeline,
Which shines here in the west.
Cymbeline. Laud we the gods;
And let our crooked smokes climb to their nostrils
From our blest altars. Publish we this peace
To all our subjects. Set we forward: let
A Roman and a British ensign wave
Friendly together; so through Lud's town march:
And in the temple of great Jupiter
Our peace we'll ratify; seal it with feasts.
Set on there! Never was a war did cease,
Ere bloody hands were wash'd, with such a peace.

SHAKESPEARE TRAGEDIES - NOTES

1. Cry havoc = signal for general slaughter
2. Petard = engine for blowing up gates
3. Shakespeare's advice to young men
4. Shakespeare's advice to fellow actors
5. Recently a well-known concert pianist died. In his youth he longed to go on the stage; but he was persuaded to concentrate on music. After his death a gruesome package arrived at the RSC at Stratford-upon-Avon from his solicitors requesting that the pianist's skull be used as 'Yorick' in productions of Hamlet. I was told at the theatre that this was done both in Stratford and London
6. Antres = caves
7. Anthropophagi = cannibals

HIGHLIGHTS FROM THE HISTORIES

KING JOHN

KING RICHARD II

KING HENRY IV (Part 1)

KING HENRY IV (Part 2)

KING HENRY V

KING HENRY VI (Part 1)

KING HENRY VI (Part 2)

KING HENRY VI (Part 3)

KING RICHARD III

KING HENRY VIII

KING JOHN

Prince Arthur to Hubert.
Have you the heart? When your head did but ache,
I knit my handkercher about your brows,
The best I had, a princess wrought it me,
And I did never ask it you again;
And with my hand at midnight held your head,
And like the watchful minutes to the hour,
Still and anon cheer'd up the heavy time,
Saying, 'What lack you?' and 'Where lies your grief?'
Or 'What good love may I perform for you?'
Many a poor man's son would have lien still
And ne'er have spoke a loving word to you;
But you at your sick service had a prince.
Nay, you may think my love was crafty love,
And call it cunning: do, an if you will:
If heaven be pleased that you must use me ill,
Why then you must. Will you put out mine eyes?
These eyes that never did nor never shall
So much as frown on you.

Salisbury. Therefore, to be possess'd with double pomp,
To guard a title that was rich before,
To gild refined gold, to paint the lily,
To throw a perfume on the violet,
To smooth the ice, or add another hue
Unto the rainbow, or with taper-light
To seek the beauteous eye of heaven to garnish,
Is wasteful and ridiculous to excess.

Bastard. By all the blood that ever fury breathed,
The youth says well. Now hear our English king;
For thus his royalty doth speak in me.

He is prepared, and reason too he should:
This apish and unmannerly approach,
This harness'd masque and unadvised revel,
This unhair'd sauciness and boyish troops,
The king doth smile at; and is well prepared
To whip this dwarfish war, these pigmy arms,
From out the circle of his territories.
That hand which had the strength, even at your door,
To cudgel you and make you take the hatch,
To dive, like buckets, in concealed wells,
To crouch in litter of your stable planks;
To lie like pawns lock'd up in chests and trunks,
To hug with swine, to seek sweet safety out
In vaults and prisons, and to thrill and shake
Even at the crying of your nation's crow,
Thinking his voice an armed Englishman;
Shall that victorious hand be feebled here,
That in your chambers gave you chastisement?
No: know the gallant monarch is in arms
And like an eagle o'er his aery towers,
To souse annoyance that comes near his nest.
And you degenerate, you ingrate revolts,
You bloody Neroes, ripping up the womb
Of your dear mother England, blush for shame;
For your own ladies and pale-visaged maids
Like Amazons come tripping after drums,
Their thimbles into armed gauntlets change,
Their needles to lances, and their gentle hearts
To fierce and bloody inclination.

V, vii

Prince Henry. At Worcester must his body be interr'd;
    For so he will'd it.
Bastard. Thither shall it then;
    And happily may your sweet self put on
    The lineal state and glory of the land!
    To whom, with all submission, on my knee

I do bequeath my faithful services
And true subjection everlastingly . . .
Prince Henry. I have a kind soul that would give you thanks
And knows not how to do it but with tears.
Bastard. O, let us pay the time but needful woe,
Since it hath been beforehand with our griefs.
This England never did, nor never shall,
Lie at the proud foot of a conqueror,
But when it first did help to wound itself.
Now these her princes are come home again,
Come the three corners of the world in arms,
And we shall shock them. Nought shall make us rue,
If England to itself do rest but true.

RICHARD II

II, iii

Mowbray. A heavy sentence, my most sovereign liege,[3]
And all unlook'd for from your highness' mouth
A dearer merit, not so deep a maim
As to be cast forth in the common air,
Have I deserved at your highness' hands.
The language I have learn'd these forty years,
My native English, now I must forgo:
And now my tongue's use is to me no more
Than an unstring'd viol or a harp:
Or like a cunning instrument cased up,
Or, being open, put into his hands
That knows no touch to tune the harmony;
Within my mouth you have engaol'd my tongue,
Doubly portcullis'd with my teeth and lips;
And dull unfeeling barren ignorance
Is made my gaoler to attend on me.
I am too old to fawn upon a nurse,
Too far in years to be a pupil now:

What is thy sentence then but speechless death,
Which robs my tongue from breathing native breath?

Gaunt. All places that the eye of heaven visits
    Are to a wise man ports and happy havens.
    Teach thy necessity to reason thus:
    There is no virtue like necessity . . .
    Look, what thy soul holds dear, imagine it
    To lie that way thou go'st, not whence thou comest:
    Suppose the singing birds musicians,
    The grass whereon thou tread'st the presence strew'd
    The flowers fair ladies, and thy steps no more
    Than a delightful measure or a dance;
    For gnarling sorrow hath less power to bite
    The man that mocks at it and sets it light.
Bolingbroke. O, who can hold a fire in his hand
    By thinking on the frosty Caucasus?
    Or cloy the hungry edge of appetite
    By bare imagination of a feast?
    Or wallow naked in December's snow
    By thinking on fantastic summer's heat?
    O, no! the apprehension of the good
    Gives but the greater feeling to the worse:
    Fell sorrow's tooth doth never rankle more
    Than when he bites, but lanceth not the sore.

II, i

Gaunt. O, but they say the tongues of dying men
    Enforce attention like deep harmony:
    Where words are scarce, they are seldom spent in vain,
    For they breathe truth that breathe their words in pain . . .
    More are men's ends mark'd than their lives before;
    The setting sun, and music at the close,
    As the last taste of sweets, is sweetest last,
    Writ in remembrance more than things long past . . .
    Methinks I am a prophet new inspired
    And thus expiring do foretell of him:

His rash fierce blaze of riot cannot last,
For violent fires soon burn out themselves;
Small showers last long, but sudden storms are short;
He tires betimes that spurs too fast betimes;
With eager feeding food doth choke the feeder: . . .
This royal throne of kings, this scepter'd isle,
This earth of majesty, this seat of Mars,
This other Eden, demi-paradise:
This fortress built by Nature for herself
Against infection and the hand of war;
This happy breed of men, this little world,
This precious stone set in the silver sea,
Which serves it in the office of a wall,
Or as a moat defensive to a house,
Against the envy of less happier lands;
This blessed plot, this earth, this realm, this England,
This nurse, this teeming womb of royal kings,
Fear'd by their breed and famous by their birth,
Renowned for their deeds as far from home,
For Christian service and true chivalry,
As is the sepulchre in stubborn Jewry
Of the world's ransom, blessed Mary's Son;
This land of such dear souls, this dear dear land,
Dear for her reputation through the world,
Is now leased out, I die pronouncing it,
Like to a tenement or pelting farm:
England, bound in with the triumphant sea,
Whose rocky shore beats back the envious siege
Of watery Neptune, is now bound in with shame,
With inky blots and rotten parchment bonds:
That England, that was wont to conquer others,
Has made a shameful conquest of itself.

III, ii

King Richard. I weep for joy
   To stand upon my kingdom once again.
   Dear earth, I do salute thee with my hand,

165

Though rebels wound thee with their horses' hoofs:
As a long-parted mother with her child
Plays fondly with her tears and smiles in meeting,
So, weeping, smiling, greet I thee, my earth,
And do thee favours, with my royal hands.
Feed not thy sovereign's foe, my gentle earth,
Nor with thy sweets comfort his ravenous sense;
But let thy spiders, that suck up thy venom,
And heavy-gaited toads lie in their way,
Doing annoyance to the treacherous feet
Which with usurping steps do trample thee:
Yield stinging nettles to mine enemies;
And when they from thy bosom pluck a flower,
Guard it, I pray thee, with a lurking adder
Whose double tongue may with a mortal touch
Throw death upon thy sovereign's enemies . . .
Discomfortable cousin! know'st thou not
That when the searching eye of heaven is hid
Behind the globe, that lights the lower world,
Then thieves and robbers range abroad unseen
In murders and in outrage, boldly here;
But when from under this terrestrial ball
He fires the proud tops of the eastern pines
And darts his light through every guilty hole,
Then murders, treasons and detested sins,
The cloak of night being pluck'd from off their backs,
Stand bare and naked, trembling at themselves? . . .
Not all the water in the rough rude sea
Can wash the balm from an anointed king;
The breath of worldly men cannot depose
The deputy elected by the Lord.

Scroop. Glad am I that your highness is so arm'd
    To bear the tidings of calamity.
    Like an unseasonable stormy day,
    Which makes the silver rivers drown their shores,
    As if the world were all dissolved to tears,

So high above his limits swells the rage
Of Bolingbroke, covering your fearful land
With hard bright steel and hearts harder than steel.
White-beards have arm'd their thin and hairless scalps
Against thy majesty; boys, with women's voices,
Strive to speak big and clap their female joints
In stiff unwieldly arms against thy crown:
Thy very beadsmen learn to bend their bows
Of double-fatal yew against thy state;
Yea, distaff-women manage rusty bills
Against thy seat: both young and old rebel,
And all goes worse than I have power to tell.

King Richard. No matter where; of comfort no man speak,
    Let's talk of graves, of worms and epitaphs;
    Make dust our paper and with rainy eyes
    Write sorrow on the bosom of the earth.
    Let's choose executors and talk of wills;
    And yet not so, for what can we bequeath
    Save our deposed bodies to the ground? . . .
    For God's sake, let us sit upon the ground
    And tell sad stories of the death of kings:
    How some have been deposed; some slain in war;
    Some haunted by the ghosts they have deposed;
    Some poison'd by their wives; some sleeping kill'd;
    All murder'd: for within the hollow crown
    That rounds the mortal temples of a king
    Keeps Death his court, and there the antic sits,
    Scoffing his state and grinning at his pomp,
    Allowing him a breath, a little scene,
    To monarchize, be fear'd and kill with looks,
    Infusing him with self and vain conceit,
    As if this flesh which walls about our life
    Were brass impregnable, and humour'd thus
    Comes at the last and with little pin
    Bores through his castle wall, and farewell king! . . .
    I live with bread like you, feel want,

Taste grief, need friends: subjected thus,
How can you say to me, I am a king?
Bishop of Carlisle. My lord, wise men ne'er sit and wail their woes,
But presently prevent the ways to wail.
To fear the foe, since fear oppresseth strength,
Gives in your weakness strength unto your foe,
And so your follies fight against yourself.
Fear, and be slain; no worse can come to fight:
And fight and die is death destroying death;
Where fearing dying pays death servile breath.

III, iii

King Richard. We are amazed; and thus long have we stood
To watch the fearful bending of thy knee,
Because we thought ourself thy lawful king:
And if we be, how dare thy joints forget
To pay their awful duty to our presence?
If we be not, show us the hand of God
That hath dismiss'd us from our stewardship;
For well we know, no hand of blood and bone
Can gripe the sacred handle of our sceptre,
Unless he do profane, steal, or usurp . . .
Yet know, my master, God omnipotent,
Is mustering in his clouds on our behalf
Armies of pestilence; and they shall strike
Your children yet unborn and unbegot,
That lift your vassal hands against my head,
And threat the glory of my precious crown.
Tell Bolingbroke . . .
                        He is come to open
The purple testament of bleeding war;
But ere the crown he looks for live in peace,
Ten thousand bloody crowns of mothers' sons
Shall ill become the flower of England's face,
Change the complexion of her maid-pale peace
To scarlet indignation, and bedew
Her pastures' grass with faithful English blood.

King Richard. What must the king do now? Must he submit?
   The king shall do it: must he be deposed?
   The king shall be contented: must he lose
   The name of king? o' God's name let it go:
   I'll give my jewels for a set of beads,
   My gorgeous palace for a hermitage,
   My gay apparel for an almsman's gown,
   My figured goblets for a dish of wood,
   My sceptre for a palmer's walking-staff,
   My subjects for a pair of carved saints,
   And my large kingdom for a little grave;
   Or I'll be buried in the king's highway,
   Some way of common trade, where subjects' feet
   May hourly trample on their sovereign's head;
   For on my heart they tread now whilst I live;
   And buried once, why not upon my head!

III, iv

Gardener. Poor Queen, so that thy state might be no worse,
   I would my skill were subject to thy curse. -
   Here did she fall a tear; here in this place
   I'll set a bank of rue, sour herb of grace:
   Rue, even for ruth, here shortly shall be seen,
   In the remembrance of a weeping queen.[4]

IV, i

King Richard. Alack, why am I sent for to a king,
   Before I have shook off the regal thoughts
   Wherewith I reign'd? I hardly yet have learn'd
   To insinuate, flatter, bow, and bend my limbs:
   Give sorrow leave awhile to tutor me
   To this submission. Yet I well remember
   The favours of these men: were they not mine?
   Did they not sometime cry 'All hail!' to me?
   So Judas did to Christ: but he, in twelve,
   Found truth in all but one; I, in twelve thousand, none,
   God save the king! Will no man say amen?

Am I both priest and clerk? well then, amen.
God save the king! although I be not he;
And yet, amen, if heaven do think him me . . .
Give me the crown . . .
                    On this side my hand, and on that side thine.
Now is the golden crown like a deep well
that owes two buckets, filling one another,
The emptier ever dancing in the air,
The other down, unseen and full of water:
That bucket down and full of tears am I,
Drinking my griefs, whilst you mount up on high . . .
Ay, no; no, ay; for I must nothing be, . . .
Now mark me, how I will undo myself:
I give this heavy weight from off my head
And this unwieldy sceptre from my hand,
The pride of kingly sway from out my heart;
With mine own tears I wash away my balm
With mine own hands I give away my crown,
With mine own tongue deny my sacred state,
With mine own breath release all duty's rites:
All pomp and majesty I do forswear;
My manors, rents, revenues I forgo;
My acts, decrees, and statutes I deny:
God pardon all oaths that are broke to me!

KING HENRY IV (Part 1)

I,iii

Hotspur. My liege, I did deny no prisoners.
    But I remember, when the fight was done,
    When I was dry with rage and extreme toil,
    Breathless and faint, leaning upon my sword,
    Came there a certain lord, neat, and trimly dress'd
    Fresh as a bridegroom; and his chin new reap'd
    Show'd like a stubble-land at harvest-home;

170

Shakespeare

He was perfumed like a milliner;
And 'twixt his finger and his thumb he held
A pouncet-box,⁵ which ever and anon
He gave his nose and took't away again;
Who therewith angry, when it next came there,
Took it in snuff; and still he smiled and talk'd,
And as the soldiers bore dead bodies by,
He called them untaught knaves, unmannerly,
To bring a slovenly unhandsome corse
Betwixt the wind and his nobility.
With many holiday and lady terms
He question'd me; amongst the rest, demanded
My prisoners in your majesty's behalf.
I then, all smarting with my wounds being cold,
To be so pester'd with a popinjay,
Out of my grief and my impatience,
Answer'd neglectingly I know not what,
He should, or he should not; for he made me mad
To see him shine so brisk, and smell so sweet
And talk so like a waiting-gentlewoman
Of guns and drums and wounds, - God save the mark! -
And telling me the sovereign'st thing on earth
Was parmaceti for an inward bruise;
And that it was great pity, so it was,
That villanous salt-petre should be digg'd
Out of the bowels of the harmless earth,
Which many a good tall fellow had destroy'd
So cowardly; and but for these vile guns,
He would himself have been a soldier.

III, i

Mortimer. I understand thy looks: that pretty Welsh
Which thou pour'st down from these swelling heavens
I am too perfect in; and, but for shame,
In such a parley should I answer thee.
I understand thy kisses and thou mine,
And that's a feeling disputation:

171

But I will never be a truant, love,
Till I have learn'd thy language; for thy tongue
Makes Welsh as sweet as ditties highly penn'd,
Sung by a fair queen in a summer's bower,
With ravishing division, to her lute . . .

Glendower. She bids you on the wanton rushes lay you down
And rest your gentle head upon her lap,
And she will sing the song that pleaseth you,
And on your eyelids crown the god of sleep,
Charming your blood with pleasing heaviness,
Making such difference 'twixt wake and sleep
As is the difference betwixt day and night
The hour before the heavenly-harness'd team
Begins his golden progress in the east.[6]

III, ii

King to Prince. God pardon thee! yet let me wonder, Harry,
At thy affections, which do hold a wing
Quite from the flight of all thy ancestors.
Thy place in council thou hast rudely lost,
Which by thy younger brother is supplied,
And art almost an alien to the hearts
Of all the court and princes of my blood:
The hope and expectation of thy time
Is ruin'd, and the soul of every man
Prophetically doth forethink thy fall.
Had I so lavish of my presence been,
So common-hackney'd in the eyes of men,
So stale and cheap to vulgar company,
Opinion, that did help me to the crown,
Had still kept loyal to possession,
And left me in reputeless banishment,
A fellow of no mark nor likelihood.
By being seldom seen, I could not stir
But like a comet I was wonder'd at;
That men would tell their children 'This is he;'

Others would say 'Where, which is Bolingbroke?'
And then I stole all courtesy from heaven,
And dress'd myself in such humility
That I did pluck allegiance from men's hearts,
Loud shouts and salutations from their mouths,
Even in the presence of the crowned king.
Thus did I keep my person fresh and new;
My presence, like a robe pontifical,
Ne'er seen but wonder'd at: and so my state,
Seldom but sumptuous, showed like a feast,
And won by rareness such solemnity.
The skipping king, he ambled up and down,
With shallow jesters and rash bavin[7] wits,
Soon kindled and soon burnt; carded[8] his state,
Mingled his royalty with capering fools,
Had his great name profaned with their scorns,
And gave his countenance, against his name,
To laugh at gibing boys, and stand the push
Of every beardless vain comparative,
Grew a companion to the common streets,
Enfeoff'd himself to popularity;
That, being daily swallow'd by men's eyes,
They surfeited with honey and began
To loathe the taste of sweetness, whereof a little
More than a little is by much too much.
Soon when he had occasion to be seen,
He was but as the cuckoo is in June,
Heard, not regarded; seen, but with such eyes
As, sick and blunted with community,
Afford no extraordinary gaze,
Such as is bent on sun-like majesty
When it shines seldom in admiring eyes; . . .

V, ii

Vernon. No, by my soul; I never in my life
  Did hear a challenge urged more modestly,
  Unless a brother should a brother dare

To gentle exercise and proof of arms.
He gave you all the duties of a man;
Trimm'd up your praises with a princely tongue,
Spoke your deservings like a chronicle,
Making you ever better than his praise
By still dispraising praise valued with you;
And, which became him like a prince indeed,
He made a blushing cital of himself;
And chid his truant youth with such a grace
As if he master'd there a double spirit
Of teaching and of learning instantly,
There did he pause: but let me tell the world,
If he outlive the envy of this day,
England did never owe so sweet a hope,
So much misconstrued in his wantonness.

KING HENRY IV (Part 2)

II, iii

Lady Percy. O yet, for God's sake, go not to these wars! . . .
There were two honours lost, yours and your son's.
For yours, the God of heaven brighten it!
For his, it stuck upon him as the sun
In the grey vault of heaven, and by his light
Did all the chivalry of England move
To do brave acts: he was indeed the glass
Wherein the noble youth did dress themselves:
He had no legs that practised not his gait;
And speaking thick, which nature made his blemish,
Became the accents of the valiant;
For those that could speak low and tardily
Would turn their own perfection to abuse
To seem like him: so that in speech, in gait,
In diet, in affections of delight,
In military rules, humours of blood,

Shakespeare

He was the mark and glass, copy and book,
That fashion'd others.

III, i

King. How many thousand of my poorest subjects
Are at this hour asleep! O sleep, O gentle sleep,
Nature's soft nurse, how have I frighted thee,
That thou no more wilt weight my eyelids down,
And steep my senses in forgetfulness?
Why rather, sleep, liest thou in smoky cribs,
Upon uneasy pallets stretching thee,
And hush'd with buzzing night-flies to thy slumber,
Than in the perfumed chambers of the great,
Under the canopies of costly state,
And lull'd with sound of sweetest melody?
O thou dull god, why liest thou with the vile
In loathsome beds, and leavest the kingly couch
A watch-case or a common 'larum bell?
Wilt thou upon the high and giddy mast
Seal up the ship-boy's eyes, and rock his brains
In cradle of the rude imperious surge,
And in the visitation of the winds,
Who take the ruffian billows by the top,
Curling their monstrous heads, and hanging them
With deafening clamour in the slippery clouds,
That, with the hurly, death itself awakes?
Canst thou, O partial sleep, give thy repose
To the wet sea-boy in an hour so rude;
And in the calmest and most stillest night,
With all appliances and means to boot,
Deny it to a king? Then happy low, lie down!
Uneasy lies the head that wears a crown.

IV, v

Prince. Why doth the crown lie there upon his pillow,
Being so troublesome a bedfellow?
O polish'd perturbation! golden care!

That keep'st the ports of slumber open wide
To many a watchful night! sleep with it now!
Yet not so sound and half so deeply sweet
As he whose brow was homely biggen bound
Snores out the watch of night. O majesty!
When thou dost pinch thy bearer, thou dost sit
Like a rich armour worn in heat of day,
That scalds with safety. By his gates of breath
There lies a downy feather which stirs not:
Did he suspire, that light and weightless down
Perforce must move. My gracious lord! my father! . . .
I never thought to hear you speak again.
King. Thy wish was father, Harry, to that thought:
I stay too long by thee, I weary thee.
Dost thou so hunger for mine empty chair
That thou wilt needs invest thee with my honours
Before thy hour be ripe? O foolish youth!
Thou seek'st the greatness that will overwhelm thee.
Stay but a little; for my cloud of dignity
Is held from falling with so weak a wind
That it will quickly drop: my day is dim.
Thou hast stolen that which after some few hours
Were thine without offence; and at my death
Thou hast seal'd up my expectation:
Thy life did manifest thou lovedst me not,
And thou wilt have me die assured of it.
Thou hidest a thousand daggers in thy thoughts,
Which thou hast whetted on thy stony heart,
To stab at half an hour of my life.
What! canst thou not forbear me half an hour?
Then get thee gone and dig my grave thyself,
And bid the merry bells ring to thine ear
That thou art crowned, not that I am dead.
Let all the tears that should bedew my hearse
Be drops of balm to sanctify thy head:
Only compound me with forgotten dust;
Give that which gave thee life unto the worms . . .

Prince. O pardon me, my liege! but for my tears,
    The moist impediments unto my speech,
    I had forestall'd this dear and deep rebuke,
    Ere you with grief had spoke and I had heard
    The course of it so far. There is your crown;
    And He that wears the crown immortally
    Long guard it yours! . . .
King. O my son,
    God put it in thy mind to take it hence,
    That thou mightst win the more thy father's love,
    Pleading so wisely in excuse of it!
    Come hither, Harry, sit thou by my bed;
    And hear, I think, the very latest counsel
    That ever I shall breathe. God knows, my son,
    By what by-paths and indirect crook'd ways
    I met this crown; and I myself know well
    How troublesome it sat upon my head.
    To thee it shall descend with better quiet,
    Better opinion, better confirmation;
    For all the soil of the achievement goes
    With me into the earth. It seem'd in me
    But as an honour snatched with boisterous hand,
    And I had many living to upbraid
    My gain of it by their assistances;
    Which daily grew to quarrel and to bloodshed,
    Wounding supposed peace: all these bold fears
    Thou see'st with peril I have answered;
    For all my reign hath been but as a scene
    Acting that argument: and now my death
    Changes the mode; for what in me was purchased,
    Falls upon thee in a more fairer sort;
    So thou the garland wear'st successively . . .
    More would I, but my lungs are wasted so
    That strength of speech is utterly denied me.
    How came I by the crown, O God forgive;
    And grant it may with thee in true peace live!

King Henry V. This new and gorgeous garment, majesty,
    Sits not so easy on me as you think.
    Brothers, you mix your sadness with some fear:
    This is the English, not the Turkish court;
    Not Amurath an Amurath succeeds,
    But Harry Harry. Yet be sad, good brothers,
    For, by my faith, it very well becomes you:
    Sorrow so royally in you appears
    That I will deeply put the fashion on,
    And wear it in my heart: why then, be sad;
    But entertain no more of it, good brothers,
    Than a joint burden laid upon us all.
    For me, by heaven, I bid you be assured,
    I'll be your father and your brother too;
    Let me but bear your love, I'll bear your cares:
    Yet weep that Harry's dead; and so will I;
    But Harry lives, that shall convert those tears
    By number into hours of happiness.

Chief Justice. I then did use the person of your father;
    The image of his power lay then in me:
    And, in the administration of his law,
    Whiles I was busy for the commonwealth,
    Your highness pleased to forget my place,
    The majesty and power of law and justice,
    The image of the king whom I presented,
    And struck me in my very seat of judgement;
    Whereon, as an offender to your father,
    I gave bold way to my authority,
    And did commit you. If the deed were ill,
    Be you contented, wearing now the garland,
    To have a son set your decrees at nought,
    To pluck down justice from your awful bench,
    To trip the course of law and blunt the sword
    That guards the peace and safety of your person; . . .

King. You are right, justice, and you weigh this well;
   Therefore still bear the balance and the sword:
   And I do wish your honours may increase,
   Till you do live to see a son of mine
   Offend you, and obey you, as I did . . .
   For which, I do commit into your hand
   The unstained sword that you have used to bear;
   With this remembrance, that you use the same
   With the like bold, just, and impartial spirit
   As you have done 'gainst me. There is my hand.
   You shall be as a father to my youth:
   My voice shall sound as you do prompt mine ear,
   And I will stoop and humble mine intents
   To your well-practised wise directions . . .
                    The tide of blood in me
   Hath proudly flow'd in vanity till now:
   Now doth it turn and ebb back to the sea,
   Where it shall mingle with the state of floods,
   And flow henceforth in formal majesty.

KING HENRY V

Prologue

Chorus. O for a Muse of fire, that would ascend
   The brightest heaven of invention,
   A kingdom for a stage, princes to act
   And monarchs to behold the swelling scene!
   Then should the warlike Harry, like himself,
   Assume the port of Mars; and at his heels,
   Leash'd in like hounds, should famine, sword and fire
   Crouch for employment. But pardon, gentles all,
   The flat unraised spirits that have dared
   On this unworthy scaffold to bring forth
   So great an object: can this cockpit hold
   The vasty fields of France? or may we cram

Within this wooden O the very casques
That did affright the air at Agincourt? . . .
Suppose within the girdle of these walls
Are now confined two mighty monarchies,
Whose high upreared and abutting fronts
The perilous narrow ocean parts asunder:
Piece out our imperfections with your thoughts;
Into a thousand parts divide one man,
And make imaginary puissance;
Think, when we talk of horses, that you see them
Printing their proud hoofs i' the receiving earth;
For 'tis your thoughts that now must deck our kings,
Carry them here and there; jumping o'er times,
Turning the accomplishments of many years
Into an hour-glass: for the which supply,
Admit me Chorus to this history;

I, ii

Archbishop of Canterbury. Therefore doth heaven divide
    the state of man in divers functions,
    Setting endeavour in continual motion;
    To which is fixed, as an aim or butt,
    Obedience: for so work the honey-bees,
    Creatures that by a rule in nature teach
    The act of order to a peopled kingdom.
    They have a king and officers of sorts;
    Where some, like magistrates, correct at home,
    Others, like merchants, venture trade abroad,
    Others, like soldiers, armed in their stings,
    Make boot upon the summer's velvet buds,
    Which pillage they with merry march bring home
    To the tent-royal of their emperor;
    Who, busied in his majesty, surveys
    The singing masons building roofs of gold,
    The civil citizens kneading up the honey,
    The poor mechanic porters crowding in
    Their heavy burdens at his narrow gate

Shakespeare

The sad-eyed justice, with his surly hum,
Delivering o'er to executors pale
The lazy yawning drone.[9]

(Shakespeare's 'Life of the Bee')

Act II Prologue

Chorus. Now all the youth of England are on fire,
  And silken dalliance in the wardrobe lies:
  Now thrive the armorers, and honour's thought
  Reigns solely in the breast of every man:
  They sell the pasture now to buy the horse,
  Following the mirror of all Christian kings,
  With winged heels, as English Mercuries.
  For now sits Expectation in the air,
  And hides a sword from hilts unto the point
  With crowns imperial, crowns and coronets,
  Promised to Harry and his followers . . .

Act II, Prologue

Chorus. Thus with imagined wing our swift scene flies
  In motion of no less celerity
  Than that of thought. Suppose that you have seen
  The well-appointed king at Hampton pier
  Embark his royalty; and his brave fleet
  With silken streamers the young Phoebus fanning:
  Play with your fancies, and in them behold
  Upon the hempen tackle ship-boys climbing;
  Hear the shrill whistle which doth order give
  To sounds confused; behold the threaden sails,
  Borne with the invisible and creeping wind,
  Draw the huge bottoms through the furrow'd sea,
  Breasting the lofty surge: O, do but think
  You stand upon the rivage and behold
  A city on the inconstant billows dancing;
  For so appears this fleet majestical,
  Holding due course to Harfleur. Follow, follow:

181

Grapple your minds to sternage of this navy,
And leave your England, as dead midnight still,
Guarded with grandsires, babies and old women,
Either past or not arrived to pith and puissance;
For who is he, whose chin is but enrich'd
With one appearing hair, that will not follow
These cull'd and choice-drawn cavaliers to France? . . .

Act III Sc.1

King. Once more into the breach, dear friends, once more
Or close the wall up with our English dead.
In peace there's nothing so becomes a man
As modest stillness and humility;
But when the blast of war blows in our ears,
Then imitate the action of the tiger;
Stiffen the sinews, summon up the blood,
Disguise fair nature with hard-favour'd rage;
Then lend the eye a terrible aspect;
Let it pry through the portage of the head
Like the brass cannon; let the brow o'erwhelm it
As fearfully as doth a galled rock
O'erhang and jutty his confounded base,
Swill'd with the wild and wasteful ocean.
Now set the teeth and stretch the nostrils wide,
Hold hard the breath and bend up every spirit
To his full height. On, on, you noblest English,
Whose blood is let from fathers of war-proof!
Fathers that, like so many Alexanders,
Have in these parts from morn to even fought,
And sheathed their swords for lack of argument;
Dishonour not your mothers; now attest
That those whom you call'd fathers did beget you
Be copy now to men of grosser blood,
And teach them how to war. And you, good yeomen,
Whose limbs were made in England, show us here
The mettle of your pasture; let us swear
That you are worth your breeding; which I doubt not;

For there is none of you so mean and base
That hath not noble lustre in your eyes.
I see you stand like greyhounds in the slips
Straining upon the start. The game's afoot;
Follow your spirit, and upon this charge
Cry "God for Harry, England and Saint George!"

Act IV Prologue

Chorus. Now entertain conjecture of a time
    When creeping murmur and the poring dark
    Fills the wide vessel of the universe,
    From camp to camp through the foul womb of night
    The hum of either army stilly sounds,
    That the fix'd sentinels almost receive
    The secret whispers of each other's watch:
    Fire answers fire, and through their paly flames
    Each battle sees the other's umber'd face;
    Steed threatens steed, in high and boastful neighs
    Piercing the night's dull ear; and from the tents
    The armorers, accomplishing the knights,
    With busy hammers closing rivets up,
    Give dreadful note of preparation:
    The country cocks do crow, the clocks do toll,
    And the third hour of drowsy morning name . . .
                 The poor condemned English,
    Like sacrifices, by their watchful fires
    Sit patiently and inly ruminate
    The morning's danger, and their gesture sad
    Investing lank-lean cheeks and war-worn coats
    Presenteth them unto the gazing moon
    So many horrid ghosts. O now, who will behold
    The royal captain of this ruin'd band
    Walking from watch to watch, from tent to tent,
    Let him cry 'Praise and glory on his head!'
    For forth he goes and visits all his host,
    Bids them good morrow with a modest smile,
    And calls them brothers, friends and countrymen.

Upon his royal face there is no note
How dread an army hath enrounded him;
Nor doth he dedicate one jot of colour
Unto the weary and all-watched night,
But freshly looks and over-bears attaint
With cheerful semblance and sweet majesty;
That every wretch, pining and pale before,
Beholding him, plucks comfort from his looks:
A largess universal like the sun
His liberal eye doth give to every one,
Thawing cold fear, that mean and gentle all
Behold, as may unworthiness define,
A little touch of Harry in the night . . .

IV, i

King. Upon the king! let us our lives, our souls,
    Our debts, our careful wives,
    Our children and our sins lay on the king!
    We must bear all. O hard condition,
    Twin-born with greatness, subject to the breath
    Of every fool, whose sense no more can feel
    But his own wringing! What infinite heart's-ease
    Must kings neglect, that private men enjoy!
    And what have kings, that privates have not too,
    Save ceremony, save general ceremony? . . .
    O ceremony, show me but thy worth! . . .
    I am a king that find thee, and I know
    'Tis not the balm, the sceptre and the ball,
    The sword, the mace, the crown imperial,
    The intertissued robe of gold and pearl,
    The farced[10] title running 'fore the king,
    The throne he sits on, nor the tide of pomp
    That beats upon the high shore of this world,
    No, not all these, thrice-gorgeous ceremony,
    Not all these, laid in bed majestical,
    Can sleep so soundly as the wretched slave,
    Who with a body fill'd and vacant mind
    Gets him to rest, cramm'd with distressful bread;

Never sees horrid night, the child of hell,
But, like a lackey, from the rise to set
Sweats in the eye of Phoebus and all night
Sleeps in Elysium; next day after dawn,
Doth rise and help Hyperion to his horse,
And follows so the ever-running year,
With profitable labour, to his grave: . . .

King. O God of battles! steel my soldiers' hearts;
Possess them not with fear; take from them now
The sense of reckoning, if the opposed numbers
Pluck their hearts from them.

IV, iii

King. If we are mark'd to die, we are enow
To do our country loss; and if to live,
The fewer men, the greatest share of honour.
God's will! I pray thee, wish not one man more.
By Jove! I am not covetous for gold,
Nor care I who doth feed upon my cost;
It yearns me not if men my garments wear;
Such outward things dwell not in my desires:
But if it be a sin to covet honour,
I am the most offending soul alive . . .
Rather proclaim it, Westmoreland, through my host,
That he which hath no stomach to this fight,
Let him depart; his passport shall be made
And crowns for convoy put into his purse:
We would not die in that man's company
That fears his fellowship to die with us.
This day is call'd the feast of Crispian:
He that outlives this day, and comes safe home,
Will stand a tip-toe when this day is named,
And rouse him at the name of Crispian.
He that shall live this day and see old age,
Will yearly on the vigil feast his neighbours,
And say, 'Tomorrow is Saint Crispian:'

Then will he strip his sleeve and show his scars,
And say, 'These wounds I had on Crispin's day!'
Old men forget; yet all shall be forgot,
But he'll remember with advantages
What feats he did that day: then shall our names
Familiar in his mouth as household words,
Harry the king, Bedford and Exeter,
Warwick and Talbot, Salisbury and Gloucester,
Be in their flowing cups freshly remember'd.
This story shall the good man teach his son;
And Crispin Crispian shall ne'er go by,
From this day to the ending of the world,
But we in it shall be remembered;
We few, we happy few, we band of brothers;
For he today that sheds his blood with me
Shall be my brother; be he ne'er so vile,
This day shall gentle his condition:
And gentlemen in England now a-bed
Shall think themselves accursed they were not here,
And hold their manhoods cheap whiles any speaks
That fought with us upon Saint Crispin's day.

V Prologue

Chorus. Vouchsafe to those that have not read the story,
   That I may prompt them . . .
Now we bear the king
Toward Calais: grant him there; there seen,
Heave him away upon your winged thoughts
Athwart the sea. Behold the English beach
Pales in the flood with men, with wives and boys,
Whose shouts and claps out-voice the deep-mouth'd sea,
Which like a mighty whiffler 'fore the king
Seems to prepare his way: so let him land,
And solemnly see him set on to London . . .
         But now behold,
In the quick forge and working-house of thought,
How London doth pour out her citizens!

The mayor and all his brethren in best sort,
Like to the senators of the antique Rome,
With the plebeians swarming at their heels,
Go forth and fetch their conquering Caesar in:

Duke of Burgundy. My duty to you both, on equal love,
    Great Kings of France and England! That I have labour'd,
    With all my wits, my pains and strong endeavours,
    To bring your most imperial majesties
    Unto this bar and royal interview,
    Your mightiness on both parts best can witness.
    Since then my office hath so far prevail'd
    That, face to face and royal eye to eye,
    You have congreeted, let it not disgrace me,
    If I demand, before this royal view,
    What rub or what impediment there is,
    Why that the naked, poor and mangled Peace,
    Dear nurse of arts, plenties and joyful births,
    Should not in this best garden of the world,
    Our fertile France, put up her lovely visage?
    Alas, she hath from France too long been chased,
    And all her husbandry doth lie on heaps,
    Corrupting in its own fertility.
    Her vine, the merry cheerer of the heart,
    Unpruned dies; her hedges even-pleach'd,[11]
    Like prisoners wildly overgrown with hair,
    Put forth disorder'd twigs; her fallow leas
    The darnel, hemlock and rank fumitory
    Doth root upon, while that the coulter rusts
    That should deracinate[12] such savagery;
    The even mead, that erst brought sweetly forth
    The freckled cowslip, burnet and green clover,
    Wanting the scythe, all uncorrected, rank,
    Conceives by idleness, and nothing teems
    But hateful docks, rough thistles, kecksies,[13] burs,
    Losing both beauty and utility.

Part IV

And as our vineyards, fallows, meads and hedges,
Defective in their natures, grow to wildness,
Even so our houses and ourselves and children
Have lost, or do not learn for want of time,
The sciences that should become our country;
But grow like savages, - as soldiers will
That nothing do but meditate on blood, -
To swearing and stern looks, diffused attire
And every thing that seems unnatural.
Which to reduce into our former favour
You are assembled; and my speech entreats
That I may know the let, why gentle Peace
Should not expel these inconveniences
And bless us with her former qualities.[14]

(Lamenting the scars of war upon the countryside.)

KING HENRY VI (Part 1)

IV, ii

Talbot. Go to the gates of Bourdeaux, trumpeter;
    Summon their general unto the wall . . .
                        Open your city-gates;
    Be humble to us; call my sovereign yours,
    And do him homage as obedient subjects;
    And I'll withdraw me and my bloody power:
    But, if you frown upon this proffer'd peace,
    You tempt the fury of my three attendants,
    Lean famine, Quartering steel, and climbing fire;
    Who in a moment even with the earth
    Shall lay your stately and air-braving towers,
    If you forsake the offer of their love.

Suffolk. O fairest beauty, do not fear nor fly!
    For I will touch thee but with reverent hands;
    I kiss these fingers for eternal peace,
    And lay them gently on thy tender side . . .
    Be not offended, nature's miracle,
    Thou art allotted to be ta'en by me:
    So doth the swan her downy cygnets save,
    Keeping them prisoner underneath her wings.

Suffolk. A dower, my lords! disgrace not so your king,
    That he should be so abject, base and poor,
    To choose for wealth and not for perfect love.
    Henry is able to enrich his queen,
    And not to seek a queen to make him rich:
    So worthless peasants bargain for their wives,
    As market-men for oxen, sheep, or horse.
    Marriage is a matter of more worth
    Than to be dealt in by attorneyship;
    Not whom we will, but whom his grace affects,
    Must be companion of his nuptial bed:
    And therefore, lords, since he affects her most
    It most of all these reasons bindeth us,
    In our opinions she should be preferr'd.
    For what is wedlock forced but a hell,
    An age of discord and continual strife?
    Whereas the contrary bringeth bliss,
    And is a pattern of celestial peace.

King. Whether it be through force of your report,
    My noble Lord of Suffolk, or for that
    My tender youth was never yet attaint
    With any passion of inflaming love,
    I cannot tell; but this I am assured,
    I feel such sharp dissension in my breast,
    Such fierce alarums both of hope and fear,

As I am sick with working of my thoughts.
Take, therefore, shipping; post, my lord, to France;
Agree to any covenants, and procure
That Lady Margaret do vouchsafe to come
To cross the seas to England, and be crown'd
King Henry's faithful and anointed queen:

V, v

Suffolk: An earl I am, and Suffolk am I called.
Be not offended, nature's miracle,
Thou art allotted to be taken by me.
So doth the swan his downy cygnets save,
Keeping them prisoner underneath his wings.
Yet, if this servile usage once offend,
Go and be free again, as Suffolk's friend
    She is going
O stay! (*Aside*) I have no power to let her pass.
My hand would free her, but my heart says no.
As plays the sund upon the glassy stream,
Twinkling another counterfeited beam,
So seems this gorgeous beauty to mine eyes.
Fain would I woo her, yet I dare not speak.
I'll call for pen and ink, and write my mind.
Fie, de la Pole, disable not thyself!
Hast not a tongue? Is she not here to hear?
Wilt thou be daunted at a woman's sight?
Ay, beauty's princely majesty is such
Confounds the tongue, and makes the senses rough.

KING HENRY VI (Part 2)

I, iii

Queen. My Lord of Suffolk, say, is this the guise,
    Is this the fashion in the court of England?
    Is this the government of Britain's isle,

And this the royalty of Albion's king?
What, shall King Henry be a pupil still
Under the surly Gloucester's governance?
Am I queen in title and in style,
And must be made a subject to a duke?
I tell thee, Pole, when in the city Tours
Thou ran'st a tilt in honour of my love,
And stole'st away the ladies' hearts of France,
I thought King Henry had resembled thee
In courage, courtship and proportion:
But all his mind is bent to holiness,
To number Ave-Maries on his beads;
His champions are the prophets and apostles,
His weapons holy saws of sacred writ,
His study is his tilt-yard, and his loves
Are brazen images of canonized saints.
I would the college of the cardinals
Would choose him pope and carry him to Rome,
And sit the triple crown upon his head:
That were a state fit for his holiness.

                                                        III, ii

Queen. Be woe for me, more wretched than he is.
What, dost thou turn away and hide thy face?
I am no loathsome leper; look on me.
What! art thou, like the adder, waxen deaf?
Be poisonous too and kill thy forlorn queen.
Is all thy comfort shut in Gloucester's tomb?
Why, then, dame Margaret was ne'er thy joy.
Erect his statuë and worship it,
And make my image but an alehouse sign.
Was I for this nigh wreck'd upon the sea,
And twice by awkward wind from England's bank
Drove back again unto my native clime?
What boded this, but well forewarning wind
Did seem to say 'Seek not a scorpion's nest,
Nor set no footing on this unkind shore?'

I will repeal thee, or, be well assured,
Adventure to be banished myself:
And banished I am, if but from thee.

KING HENRY VI (Part 3)

II, ii

Clifford. My gracious liege, this too much lenity[1]
And harmful pity must be laid aside,
To whom do lions cast their gentle looks?
Not to the beast that would usurp their den.
Whose hand is that the forest bear doth lick?
Not his that spoils her young before her face.
Who 'scapes the lurking serpent's mortal sting?
Not he that sets his foot upon her back.
The smallest worm will turn being trodden on,
And doves will peck in safeguard of their brood . . .
Unreasonable creatures feed their young;
And though man's face be fearful to their eyes,
Yet, in protection of their tender ones,
Who hath not seen them, even with those wings
Which sometime they have used with fearful flight,
Make war with him that climb'd unto their nest,
Offering their own lives in their young's defence?

II, v

King. This battle fares like to the morning's war,[2]
When dying clouds contend with growing light,
What time the shepherd, blowing of his nails,
Can neither call it perfect day nor night.
Now sways it this way, like a mighty sea
Forced by the tide to combat with the wind;
Now sways it that way, like the selfsame sea
Forced to retire by fury of the wind:
Sometime the flood prevails, and then the wind;
Now one the better, then another best;

Both tugging to be victors, breast to breast,
Yet neither conqueror nor conquered:
So is the equal poise of this fell war.
Here on this molehill will I sit me down.
To whom God will, there be the victory!
For Margaret my queen, and Clifford too,
Have chid me from the battle; swearing both
They prosper best of all when I am thence.
Would I were dead! if God's good will were so;
For what is in this world but grief and woe?
O God! methinks it were a happy life,
To be no better than a homely swain;
To sit upon a hill, as I do now,
To carve out dials quaintly, point by point,
Thereby to see the minutes how they run,
How many make the hour full complete;
How many hours bring about the day;
How many days will finish up the year;
How many years a mortal man may live.
When this is known, then to divide the times:
So many hours must I tend my flock;
So many hours must I take my rest;
So many hours must I contemplate;
So many hours must I sport myself;
So many days my ewes have been with young;
So many weeks ere the poor fools will ean;
So many years ere I shall shear the fleece:
So minutes, hours, days, months, and years,
Pass'd over to the end they were created,
Would bring white hairs unto a quiet grave.
Ah! what a life were this! how sweet! how lovely!
Gives not the hawthorn-bush a sweeter shade
To shepherds looking on their silly sheep,
Than doth a rich embroider'd canopy
To kings that fear their subjects' treachery?
O, yes, it doth; a thousand-fold it doth
And to conclude, the shepherd's homely curds,

His cold thin drink out of his leather bottle,
His wonted sleep under a fresh tree's shade,
All which secure and sweetly he enjoys,
Is far beyond a prince's delicates,
His viands sparkling in a golden cup,
His body couched in a curious bed,
When care, mistrust, and treason waits on him.

III, ii

Gloucester. Ay, Edward will use women honourably.
  Would he were wasted, marrow, bones and all,
  That from his loins no hopeful branch may spring,
  To cross me from the golden time I look for! . . .
  Like one that stands upon a promontory,
  And spies a far-off shore where he would tread,
  Wishing his foot were equal with his eye,
  And chides the sea that sunders him from thence,
  Saying, he'll lade it dry to have his way:
  So do I wish the crown, being so far off;
  And so I chide the means that keeps me from it;
  And so I say, I'll cut the causes off,
  Flattering me with impossibilities . . .
  Well, say there is no kingdom then for Richard;
  What other pleasures can the world afford?
  I'll make my heaven in a lady's lap,
  And deck my body in gay ornaments,
  And witch sweet ladies with my words and looks . . .
  Then, since this earth affords no joy to me, . . .
  I'll make my heaven to dream upon the crown,
  And, whiles I live, to account this world but hell,
  Until my mis-shaped trunk that bears this head
  Be round impaled with a glorious crown . . .
  I'll drown more sailors than the mermaid shall;
  I'll slay more gazers than the basilisk;
  I'll play the orator as well as Nestor,
  Deceive more slily than Ulysses could,
  And, like a Sinon, take another Troy.

I can add colours to the chameleon,
Change shapes with Proteus for advantages,
And set the murderous Machiavel to school.

V, ii

Warwick. Ah, who is nigh? come to me, friend or foe, . . .
My blood, my want of strength, my sick heart shows,
That I must yield my body to the earth,
And, by my fall, the conquest to my foe,
Thus yields the cedar to the axe's edge
Whose arms gave shelter to the princely eagle,
Under whose shade the ramping lion slept,
Whose top-branch overpeer'd Jove's spreading tree,
And kept low shrubs from winter's powerful wind.
These eyes, that now are dimm'd with death's black veil,
Have been as piercing as the mid-day sun,
To search the secret treasons of the world:
The wrinkles in my brows, now fill'd with blood,
Were liken'd oft to kingly sepulchres;
For who lived king, but I could dig his grave?
And who durst smile when Warwick bent his brow?
Lo, now my glory smear'd in dust and blood!
My parks, my walks, my manors that I had,
Even now forsake me, and of all my lands
Is nothing left me but my body's length.

V, iv

Queen Margaret. Great lords, wise men ne'er sit and wail their loss,
But cheerly seek how to redress their harms.
What though the mast be now blown overboard,
The cable broke, the holding-anchor lost,
And half our sailors swallow'd in the flood?
yet lives our pilot still. Is't meet that he
Should leave the helm, and like a fearful lad
With tearful eyes add water to the sea,
And give more strength to that which hath too much,
Whiles, in his moan, the ship splits on the rock,

Part IV

Which industry and courage might have saves? . . .
Why, courage then! what cannot be avoided
'Twere childish weakness to lament or fear.

RICHARD III

I, i

Gloucester. Now is the winter of our discontent
    Made glorious summer by this son of York;
    And all the clouds that lour'd upon our house
    In the deep bosom of the ocean buried.
    Now are our brows bound with victorious wreaths;
    Our bruised arms hung up for monuments;
    Our stern alarms changed to merry meetings,
    Our dreadful marches to delightful measures
    Grim-visaged war hath smooth'd his wrinkled front;
    And now, instead of mounting barbed steeds
    To fright the souls of fearful adversaries,
    He capers nimbly in a lady's chamber
    To the lascivious pleasing of a lute.
    But I, that am not shaped for sportive tricks,
    Nor made to court an amorous looking-glass;
    I, that am rudely stamp'd, and want love's majesty
    To strut before a wanton ambling nymph;
    I, that am curtail'd of this fair proportion,
    Cheated of feature by dissembling nature,
    Deform'd, unfinish'd, sent before my time
    Into this breathing world, scarce half made up
    And that so lamely and unfashionable
    That dogs bark at me as I halt by them;
    Why, I, in this weak piping time of peace,
    Have no delight to pass away the time,
    Unless to spy my shadow in the sun,
    And descant on mine own deformity:
    And therefore, since I cannot prove a lover,

To entertain these fair well-spoken days,
I am determined to prove a villain,
And hate the idle pleasures of these days.

III,vii

Buckingham. Then know, it is your fault that you resign
    The supreme seat, the throne majestical,
    The scepter'd office of your ancestors,
    Your state of fortune and your due of birth,
    The lineal glory of your royal house,
    To the corruption of a blemish'd stock:
    Whilst, in the mildness of your sleepy thoughts,
    Which here we waken to our country's good,
    This noble isle doth want her proper limbs;
    Her face defaced with scars of infamy,
    Her royal stock graft with ignoble plants,
    And almost shoulder'd in the swallowing gulf
    Of blind forgetfulness and dark oblivion.
    Which to recure, we heartily solicit
    Your gracious self to take on you the charge
    And kingly government of this your land;
    Not as protector, steward, substitue,
    Or lowly factor for another's gain;
    But as successively, from blood to blood,
    Your right of birth, your empery, your own.
Gloucester. I know not whether to depart in silence,
    Or bitterly to speak in your reproof,
    Best fitteth my degree or your condition:
    If not to answer, you might haply think
    Tongue-tied ambition, not replying, yielded
    To bear the golden yoke of sovereignty,
    Which fondly you would here impose on me: . . .
    Your love deserves my thanks, but my desert
    Unmeritable shuns your high request.
    First, if all obstacles were cut away
    And that my path were even to the crown,
    As my ripe revenue and due by birth;

Yet so much is my poverty of spirit,
So mighty and so many my defects,
As I had rather hide me from my greatness,
Being a bark to brook no mighty sea,
Than in my greatness covet to be hid,
And in the vapour of my glory smother'd.

IV, iv

King Richard. Look, what is done cannot be now amended:
  Men shall deal unadvisedly sometimes,
  Which after-hours give leisure to repent.
  If I did take the kingdom from your sons,
  To make amends, I'll give it to your daughter . . .
  A grandam's name is little less in love
  Than is the doting title of a mother;
  They are as children but one step below,
  Even of your mettle, of your very blood;
  Of all one pain, save for a night of groans
  Endured of her, for whom you bid like sorrow
  Your children were vexation to your youth,
  But mine shall be a comfort to your age.
  The loss you have is but a son being king,
  And by that loss your daughter is made queen . . .
  Dorset your son, that with a fearful soul
  Leads discontented steps in foreign soil,
  This fair alliance quickly shall call home
  To high promotions and great dignity:
  The king, that calls your beauteous daughter wife,
  Familiarly shall call thy Dorset brother;
  Again shall you be mother to a king,
  And all the ruins of distressful times
  Repair'd with double riches of content,
  What! we have many goodly days to see:
  The liquid drops of tears that you have shed
  Shall come again, transform'd to orient pearl,
  Advantaging their loan with interest
  Of ten times double gain of happiness.

Go then, my mother, to thy daughter go;
Make bold her bashful years with your experience;
Prepare her ears to hear a wooer's tale;
Put in her tender heart the aspiring flame
Of golden sovereignty; acquaint the princess
With the sweet silent hours of marriage joys: . . .
Bound with triumphant garlands will I come,
And lead thy daughter to a conqueror's bed;
To whom I will retail my conquest won,
And she shall be sole victress, Caesar's Caesar.

KING HENRY VIII

I, i

Norwich. Be advised;
  Heat not a furnace for your foe so hot
That it do singe yourself: we may outrun,
By violent swiftness, that which we run at,
And lose by over-running. Know you not,
The fire that mounts the liquor till't run o'er
In seeming to augment it wastes it? Be advised:
I say again, there is no English soul
More stronger to direct you than yourself,
If with the sap of reason you would quench,
Or but allay, the fire of passion.

II, iii

Anne. Verily,
  I swear, 'tis better to be lowly born,
And range with humble livers in content
Than to be perk'd up in a glistering grief
And wear a golden sorrow.

III, ii

Wolsey. Farewell! a long farewell to all my greatness!

199

Part IV

This is the state of man: to-day he puts forth
The tender leaves of hopes; tomorrow blossoms,
And bears his blushing honours thick upon him;
The third day comes a frost, a killing frost,
And, when he thinks, good easy man, full surely
His greatness is a-ripening, nips his root,
And then he falls, as I do. I have ventured,
Like little wanton boys that swim on bladders,
This many summers in a sea of glory,
But far beyond my depth: my high-blown pride
At length broke under me, and now has left me,
Weary and old with service, to the mercy
Of a rude stream that must for ever hide me.
Vain pomp and glory of this world, I hate ye:
I feel my heart new open'd. O, how wretched
Is that poor man that hangs on princes' favours!
There is, betwixt that smile we would aspire to,
That sweet aspect of princes, and their ruin,
More pangs and fears than wars or women have:
And when he falls, he falls like Lucifer,
Never to hope again.

Wolsey. Cromwell, I did not think to shed a tear
In all my miseries; but thou hast forced me,
Out of thy honest truth, to play the woman.
Let's dry our eyes: and thus far hear me, Cromwell;
And, when I am forgotten, as I shall be,
And sleep in dull cold marble, where no mention
Of me more must be heard of, say, I taught thee;
Say, Wolsey, that once trod the ways of glory,
And sounded all the depths and shoals of honour,
Found thee a way, out of his wreck, to rise in;
A sure and safe one, though thy master miss'd it . . .
Had I but served my God with half the zeal
I served my king, he would not in mine age
Have left me naked to mine enemies.

Griffith. At last, with easy roads, he came to Leicester,[15]
  Lodged in the abbey; where the reverend abbot,
  With all his covent, honourably received him;
  To whom he gave these words, 'O father abbot,
  An old man, broken with the storms of state,
  Is come to lay his weary bones among ye;
  Give him a little earth for charity!' . . .
                This cardinal,
  Though from an humble stock, undoubtedly
  Was fashion'd to much honour from his cradle.
  He was a scholar, and a ripe and good one;
  Exceeding wise, fair-spoken and persuading:
  Lofty and sour to them that loved him not,
  But to those men that sought him, sweet as summer . . .
  He was most princely: ever witness for him
  Those twins of learning that he raised in you,
  Ipswich and Oxford! one of which fell with him, . . .
  The other, though unfinish'd, yet so famous,
  So excellent in art and still so rising,
  That Christendom shall ever speak his virtue.
  His overthrow heap'd happiness upon him;
  For then, and not till then, he felt himself,
  And found the blessedness of being little:
  And, to add greater honours to his age
  Than man could give him, he died fearing God.

Cranmer. Let me speak, sir,
  For heaven now bids me; and the words I utter
  Let none think flattery, for they'll find 'em truth.
  This royal infant - heaven still move about her! -
  though in her cradle, yet now promises
  Upon this land a thousand thousand blessings,
  Which time shall bring to ripeness: she shall be -
  But few now living can behold that goodness -
  A pattern to all princes living with her,

And all that shall succeed: Saba was never
More covetous of wisdom and fair virtue
Than this pure soul shall be: all princely graces,
That mould up such a mighty piece as this is,
With all the virtues that attend the good,
Shall still be doubled on her: truth shall nurse her,
Holy and heavenly thoughts still counsel her:
She shall be loved and fear'd: her own shall bless her;
Her foes shake like a field of beaten corn,
And hang their heads with sorrow. Good grows with her:
In her days every man shall eat in safety,
Under his own vine, what he plants, and sing
The merry songs of peace to all his neighbours:
God shall be truly known; and those about her
From her shall read the perfect ways of honour,
And by those claim their greatness, not by blood.[16]

(Extolling the future Queen Elizabeth I).

SHAKESPEARE HISTORIES - NOTES

1. Lenity = mercy
2. In this noble soliloquy Shakespeare repeats a favourite theme that the simple life of a poor man is happier than that of a monarch burdened with affairs of state - see *As You Like It* and *Henry IV* Act II, Sc i
3. The poignant cry of refugees and exiles down the ages, even unto now
4. A gem of compassion
5. A pouncet-box = perforated for perfume
6. A touching interlude
7. Bavin (wits) = a faggot of brushwood
8. Carded (his state) = adulterated
9. Shakespeare's 'Life of the Bee'
10. Farced (title) = *stuffed* with exaggeration
11. even-pleached = neatly intertwined
12. deracinate = uproot
13. kecksies = dry stems of hemlock
14. Lamenting the scars of war upon the countryside
15. Wolsey died in the abbey at Leicester, leaving his name to a brand of knitwear where it is manufactured
16. Extolling the future Queen Elizabeth I

Favourite Sonnets: 18, 30, 34, 37, 54, 55, 57, 60, 64, 66, 65, 73, 87, 94, 104, 106, 107, 116, 128, 97.

Part IV

Others abide our question – Thou art free!
We ask and ask – Thou smilest and art still,
Out-topping knowledge! So some sovran hill
Who to the stars uncrowns his majesty,
Planting his steadfast footsteps in the sea,
    Making the heaven of heavens his dwelling-place,
    Spares but the border, often, of his base
To the foil'd searching of mortality;
And thou, whose head did stars and sunbeams know,
    Self-school'd, self-scann'd, self-honour'd, self-secure,
Didst walk on earth unguess'd at. – Better so!
    All pains the immortal spirit must endure,
All weakness which impairs, all griefs which bow,
Find their sole voice in that victorious brow

Matthew Arnold
Rugby 1822–1888

Wordsworth penned the stirring sonnet below in 1802 when England was threatened with invasion by Napoleon.

It is not to be thought of that the Flood
Of British freedom, which, to the open sea
Of the world's praise, from dark antiquity
Hath flowed, 'with pomp of waters, unwithstood,'
Roused though it be full often to a mood
Which spurns the check of salutary bands,
That this most famous Stream in bogs and sands
Should perish; and to evil and to good
Be lost for ever. In our halls is hung
Armoury of the invincible knights of old:
We must be free or die, who speak the tongue
That Shakespeare spake; the faith and morals hold
Which Milton held – In every thing we are sprung
Of Earth's first blood, have titles manifold.

William Wordsworth
1770–1850

Part V

Interesting Derivations

INTERESTING DERIVATIONS

Herewith a further research into the English language. I have preferred items with an element of surprise or curiosity which I have gathered during tours of Europe with lecturers, from travel and history books and other sources. Some are only probable and you are welcome to sprinkle a little salt where it is needed. I owe much to my wife for acting as referee in the compilation of all my collections.

DERIVATIONS:

ACCORDING TO HOYLE: Edmond Hoyle in the 18th Century published rules for whist and other games and was quoted as an authority to settle doubts about any games.

ABOVE BOARD: not playing cards from under the table where cheating is possible.

ALBATROSS: from Portuguese for 'large pelican' - the subject of Coleridge's 'Ancient Mariner'.

ALERT/ALARM: Throughout history Italy has suffered from invasions or internal strife between dukedoms, even between cities. When the enemy is expected a sentinel is ordered to the watchtower or high point (*It - All'erta*) who calls: 'To Arms!' (*It - All'Arme*) when the enemy is sighted.

ALBUM: White tablet (L *albus* = white).

ALIVE AND KICKING: used in 18th Century by London fishmongers when recommending their fresh fish.

AMMONIA: Camels were parked outside the temple of Ammon, the god of Ancient Egypt, while their owners worshipped within. Urine left by the camels was scooped up by people who used this 'salt of Ammon' for bleaching.

AMAZON: from Greek 'a' (without) 'mazos' (breast) naming a tribe of female warriors who removed one breast in order to draw bow-strings. Boadicea, Queen

207

of Ancient Britons, is supposed to have done so when fighting the Romans.

ARMED TO THE TEETH: referred originally to pirates who carried their cutlasses when boarding ships (Note: In 'Eugenie Grandet' Balzac describes guests arriving: 'En*dimanchés* Jusqu'aux dents' = dressed in their Sunday best.)

ARTESIAN WELLS: after French province of *Artois*, where they were first constructed.

AUSPICIOUS: from the Roman auspex (Latin: avis = a bird and specore = to look at), the bird watcher whose duty was to observe their flight, food, entrails and habits to deduce favourable omens for the future.

BACHELOR/SPINSTER: As an unmarried daughter was formerly expected to work the *spinning wheel*, so a French farmer's unmarried son had the task of tending the cows (les vâches) as a '*vâchelor*' or as we say - *bachelor*.

BAYONET: The soldier's weapon first made in *Bayonne*, France.

BETTER HALF: quoted by Sir Philip Sidney (16th Century) to mean either spouse in marriage. Later used by Dickens in whose time it meant the wife.

BANK: from Italian Banca = the bench in a market place where money lenders conducted their trade. Any who failed were required to break their benches - in Latin 'banca rupta'.

BAKER'S DOZEN: In Medieval times there was a strict law against supplying underweight loaves so, to be on the safe side, bakers provided an extra one to the twelve charged.

BACK TO SQUARE ONE: Before the coming of television the BBC used to publish a diagram of a Rugby football pitch in the Radio Times divided into 8 squares, numbers 1 and 2 at one end and 7 and 8 at the other. This enabled listeners to follow the game with the commentator. When one side advanced from squares 1 or 2, the opposing full-back would kick the ball back over the heads of the charging forwards who would have to retreat 'back to square one' where it found touch. Similarly, 'back to the drawing board' implies a fresh start after the failure of a project.

BAR: (in law and refreshment), Shakespeare used this word for tavern because bars were erected at closing time to terminate service. The same device was used in early law courts where barristers were 'called to the Bar'.

BASTARD: (Latin 'bastum' = pack-saddle) Medieval horsemen used their pack-saddles for beds on their travels and 'misadventures'.

BEDLAM: short for St Mary of *Bethlehem*'s Hospital for the mad in London. See notes.

BERSERK: *bearskin* (*serk* = jacket) worn by ancient, frenzied warriors of Scandinavia.

BISCUIT: from the French - *Bis* (twice) *cuit* (cooked).

BITTER END: One of many expressions natural to a race of mariners. The anchor line in old ships terminated in a device to keep the rope end firmly attached to the vessel when the anchor was fully paid out. It was called the 'bitt'. The phrase has come to mean final end of hope or death.

BENDIGO, Australia, was named after an English pugilist nicknamed 'Abed-Nego' owing to his evangelical activities.

BIGWIG: The fashion set by the 'sun king' of France, Louis XIV, was copied by VIPs in Britain and continues to be worn by lawyers, speakers and certain high officials.

BILLYCAN: from the Aboriginal word 'billa' = water and the can in which it is boiled to make tea, etc.

BLACKLIST: made by Charles II of those responsible for condemning his father to death. Some were executed, others were imprisoned for life.

BLUE JEANS: from cloth woven in medieval Genoa (shortened to 'jean') to provide hard-wearing trousers, blue in colour.

BRING HOME THE BACON: The 'Dunmow Flitch' (a side of bacon) is the prize awarded to the most convincing couple who swear that they have not quarrelled over the past year. The expression now applies generally to men who bring home a prize or a good income. The ceremony has taken place at the church at Dunmow, Essex, since medieval times. (Mentioned by Chaucer)

BOWLER HAT: In the middle of last century the great agriculturalist, Thomas Coke (later Earl of Leicester) heard complaints that the beaters at the estate shoots were banging their heads on the low branches of trees. They requested hard hats which were duly designed by *Mr Bowler*, a hatter of Leicester.

BOYCOTT: name of 19th Century Irish land agent who was ignored by taxpayers in his area.

BUTTERFLY: so named by naturalists who first noticed these mainly yellow insects.

CALCULATE: The Romans used pebbles (L *calculus*) for counting - as do cricket umpires.

CANDIDATE: from Latin '*candidus*' = white, the colour of togas worn by Romans seeking office to indicate unblemished, candid character.

CALIFORNIA: named from Spanish (Mexican) for '*hot oven*' - perhaps indicating its climate.

CANOPY: Greek for mosquito net (*Konops* = gnat).

CANARY ISLANDS: where Romans found large dogs (L *canis*).

CANTALOUPE: Melons were first grown in Europe at *Cantaluppi* near Rome.

CANTANKEROUS: ill-tempered, contrary etc. from the play 'She Stoops To Conquer' by Oliver Goldsmith in the 18th Century.

CAN'T HOLD A CANDLE TO: Before cities had adequate street lighting poor fellows used to earn a little money by guiding people along the streets holding candles. Many were of poor intellect and got lost and were therefore not able to do this simple task.

CARDINAL: A VIP on whose decision events depend or turn - L *'cardo'* = hinge.

CARICATURE: Italian for heavy load (*caricare* - to load = exaggerate).

CASTANETS: generally made of chestnut wood (Gk *Kastanea* L castanea).

CHAPEL: CHAPLAIN: After St Martin, who met a poor naked beggar and cut his cloak (*cappella*) in half and gave one half to clothe him. After St Martin's death in 400 AD he became the patron saint of the Franks who treated the half-cloak as a relic which was guarded by soldiers known as cappellini or in French 'chapelain'.

CHEAT: from *'escheators'*, feudal tax collectors said to be unscrupulous in claiming heavy dues from estates rightly owing to inheritors.

CLUE: or clew (ball of thread). This 'police' word originates from Greek mythology because Ariadne attached thread along the corridors of the Maze in Crete so that Theseus could find his way to the centre, slay the Minotaur and return to safety. 'Clue' now implies a lead to the solution of a crime or puzzle.

COMIC: from Greek *'komos'* = revel.

CEMETERY: from the Greek word for dormitory - where we sleep for ever. (without) COMPUNCTION: (having no) pricking of conscience (L *punct* = pricked).

Put on the *CARPET*: At Newmarket HQ of the Jockey Club where racing wrong-doers stood on the carpet in front of the table for questioning; also members of the forces in Orderly Room.

COMRADE: In the 17th Century Spanish soldiers occupied chambers called *camaradas*, several to a room, instead of barracks.

CONTEMPLATE: from Latin '*templum*' = place for reflection (temple).

CORRIDOR: area for running along (L. It. *correre* = to run).

CORRODE: from Latin '*rodere*' = to gnaw (as rodent).

COVERLET: from Fr. '*couvrir-lit*' = cover bed.

COSTERMONGER: from Latin '*costard*' = large ribbed apple and '*monger*' (dealer).

COUPON: piece cut off (Fr. '*couper*' = to cut).

COUNTRY: from Latin '*contra*' = opposite and '*terra*' = land.

CRONY: A long-standing friend (Gk '*khronos*' = time).

CONSTABLE: from 5th Century Latin '*comes stabuli*' = master of the stables or cavalry commander which, in England, came to mean an officer at court and in command of the nation's forces and in due course a police officer.

DAINTY: HUMBLE: QUARRY: All three words derive from the French traditional hunting of deer ('*daim*' pronounced 'dan'). When a kill was made the huntsmen gave the choice (dainty) cuts to the nobles and gentry while the peasants received the offals including the umbilical (humble) cord. Finally, the remains were parcelled into the hide ('*cuirée*' = quarry) for the benefit of the hounds.

DAISY: from Day's eye which closes at night and reopens its petals in daytime.

DANDELION: lion's tooth (L '*dens leonis*').

DENIMS: serge cloth of *Nîmes*, France, where it was first made for clothing.

DEAR ME: '*Dio me* salvi!' Italian for 'God save me!'.

DECIBEL: unit to measure noise, after Alexander Bell who invented the telephone.

DERRICK: Hoisting machinery named after the London Hangman c. 1600.

DIPLOMA: Greek for 'letter folded-double' to be carried between states by diplomats.

DIRGE: The medieval funeral song based upon the verse from Psalm V commencing - '*Dirige*, Domine etc.'

DIESEL: Dr Rudolph Diesel invented the engine, using the heavy-duty oil, in Krupp's factory at Essen a century ago.
'I don't give (or care) a DAM': 'dam' = Indian coin of little value.

DELIRIUM: is based upon the Latin for ploughed ridges in fields, '*lerae*'. If they have been ploughed irregularly the ploughman was a 'delirus', who was unable to make straight furrows i.e. not concentrating, etc.

DESULTORY: from L '*salire*' = to leap. Circus riders in Ancient Rome used to jump from one horse to another in the ring. Similarly some people are prone to jump from one subject to another in conversation.

DISMAL: med. Latin '*dies mali*' = two days in each month considered unpropitious.
DISASTER: from unfavourable aspect of the stars (L '*astra*').

DISHEVELLED: untidy hair (Fr. '*cheval*' = hair).

DITTO: from It. '*detto*' = said, for recurring items in books of Florentine bankers in the 16th Century.

DOLLAR: named from old German silver coin, the '*thaler*', from metal mined in the Joachimtal ('tal' = valley).

DUCAT: coin minted by Norman *Duke* who conquered S. Italy in the 11th Century.

DUNCE: after John *Duns* Scotus, 13th Century schoolman ridiculed as the enemy of learning.

DRACONIAN: describing severe laws and punishments devised by *Draco*, Greek statesman in 600 BC.

DUPE: The hoopoe bird (in French 'huppe') has the irresponsible habit of laying its eggs in any sort of hollow except a nest. Thus a gullible person was said to have a tête d'huppe, which was shortened in English to 'dupe'.

EPICURE: *Epicurus*, Athenian philosopher of refined taste (300 BC).

ESCAPE: from Latin '*ex*' = out of and '*cappa*' = a cloak; implying that a felon who is held by the collar escapes by shedding his coat.

EXCRUCIATING: from Latin 'crucifigere' = to crucify. The Romans considered that crucifixion was the most cruel form of execution.

EXPEDITE: from Latin for foot = 'pes,*pedis*'. It implies that feet are unshackled so that one can proceed on urgent business.

FILBERT: nut due to ripen about 20th August - St *Philbert's* Day.

FLY OFF THE HANDLE: from the outburst of anger when the ill-fitting axe-head flew from the handle wielded by pioneering US frontiersmen, according to Thomas Haliburton ('Sam Slick'), mid 19th Century.

FOOLSCAP: watermark of original paper depicted a jester wearing a *fool's cap*.

FORLORN HOPE: from Dutch '*verloren*' = lost and '*hoop*' = troop or company of soldiers.

FLORIN: coin minted in Renaissance *Florence*.

FREE LANCE: the name given by Sir W. Scott in Ivanhoe to mercenary cavalry men who were skilled with the lance. Now used by self-employed journalists, etc.

FRESH: in sense of young women warning men 'don't get fresh with me', from German '*frech*' = insolent, cheeky. Probably taken by emigrants to USA.

GALAXY: from the Greek for 'milk', referring to the cluster of stars forming the Milky Way.

GAMBIT: Italian '*gambetta*' = tripping up ('gamba' = leg).

GARTER: The order of the GARTER: This order of chivalry became the most prestigious after it was instituted by Edward III. The king was dancing with the Countess of Salisbury at a royal ball when her garter fell off. He picked it up and put it on his own leg to save her from embarrassment. At the same time he declared 'Honi soit qui mal y pense' (shame to one who thinks evil of it) which became the order's motto and is embroidered in gold upon a ribbon or dark blue velvet to be worn as a garter among the knight's regalia.

GATE-CRASHING: After the departure of the Romans, British roads fell into poor condition until the 18th - 19th centuries when a series of main roads was started. The more important ones had toll houses at intervals where custodians charged tolls from the traffic to pay for road maintenance. Sometimes horsemen took a running jump over the gates standing across the highway to avoid payment until a revolving rod bearing 'pikes' was placed over the gates. This was *turned* with the (s)*pikes* pointing upward to discourage such cheating; hence the name - TURNPIKE ROAD.

GAVOTTE: dignified dance from *Gavot* in the Alps.

GAZETTE: from Venetian coin '*gazeta*' which was the price of a news sheet listing public announcements.

GENUINE: a father used to place a new born baby upon his knee (Fr. '*genu*') to acknowledge it as his.

GERRYMANDER: to manipulate boundaries for political advantage - after Governor *Gerry* of Massachusetts. The altered map of this state resembled the outline of a *salamander* in 1812.

GHETTO: an area in Venice where ammunition was once made (It. *'gettare'* = to throw) until the manufacture was moved to the new Arsenal. The Jews were obliged to occupy the vacated area in the 16th Century. The Hebrew *'ghet'* = separation, may have derived from this.

GAUZE: the filmy fabric named after *Gaza* in Palestine where it was first made.

GLADIOLUS: from the Latin 'gladius' = sword, because the Romans noticed that the long slender stem and florets resembled the sword used by gladiators in the arena.

GROG: from *'grosgrain'*, a French coarse grain material used to make a cloak for Admiral Vernon, earning him the nickname *'Grogram'*. In 1740 he ordered hot water to be poured into empty rum casks and then served to his sailors instead of neat rum, whereupon he was called 'Old Grog'.

GROTESQUE: In 16th Century Rome, antiquarians were excavating Nero's palace, which had sunk underground, when they discovered rooms or 'caves' (It. *'grotti'*) with weird paintings on the walls. They invited leading artists (including Raphael) to view them and to comment; they were declared to be *'grotto-esque'*.

GYMNASIUM: from Greek *'gymnazo'* = to train naked, because the Ancient Greeks considered that young men's athletics, performed in the nude, were an important part of their education.

HALLMARK: *mark* used at Goldsmith's *Hall* and in other UK assay offices for certifying standards of precious metals.

HAUL OVER THE COALS: torture of heretics in the 16th Century; now to reprimand wrongdoers.

HAYWIRE: when the wire tightly bound round bales of hay is carelessly cut by the farmer it is prone to fly in all directions to people nearby. The word now applies to people who are enraged or 'fly off the handle'.

HERMETIC: (sealing) from *Hermes*, the messenger of the gods, who founded alchemy using fusion, etc.

HOOLIGAN: the surname of a rowdy family of SE London.

HYPOCRITE: Greek for actor, which has come to mean a person who often behaves or pretends in a way different from his true self.

INIMICAL: hostile, from Latin *'non-amicus'* = no friend.

INFANTRY: based upon Latin *'in fans'* = unable to speak, such as babies, which was stretched to mean youths and then the Romans used the word to mean young soldiers, too inexperienced to join the cavalry.

INFLUENZA: In Renaissance Florence there was much interest in arts and sciences including astrology. The Florentines believed that the movement of the stars had a bearing upon conditions on Earth. So, if you met a friend on a cold winter's day who had a feverish cold, you would greet him with: 'Ah, I see you are under the *influence.*'

INK: from *'en-caustic'* = purple ink used for signature by Roman emperors, so that their edicts were indelible.

INVEIGLE: entice blindly (Fr. *'veuglé'* = blind).

IODINE: from Greek *'iodes'* = violet-like - the colour of iodine fumes.

IOTA: Greek for *jot.*

JEEP: short for *G*eneral *P*urpose *V*ehicle.

JEOPARDY: from the French *'jeu parti'*, a chess term meaning a divided game wherein the players are at risk of losing (16th Century).

JOURNEY: distance travelled in one day; Fr. *'journée'* L. 'diurnus'.

JOVIAL: merry characters if born under the influence of the planet Jupiter (*Jove*).

Part V

JUMBO: This Swahili word means 'chief' and was applied to a very big elephant taken from Africa to the London Zoo. It now means anything extra large.

KIDNAP: nab - kid (take child - or young goat?).

KICK THE BUCKET: formerly a method of committing suicide by standing on an upturned bucket, tying a suspended rope round the neck, then kicking the bucket away.

KERCHIEF: cover head, Fr. *'couvrir'* = to cover and *'chief'* = head.

KNAPSACK: small, strong pouch usually for soldier's rations as part of his kit on active service - from the German 'knapper' = to eat.

LACONIC: the word of Ancient Greeks of *Laconia* who were noted for their brief, brusque manner of speech as becomes their Spartan life style.

LADY: the woman who kneads dough - Old English *'hlaf'* = loaf and *'dig'* = knead.

LAVISH: from Old French 'lavasse' = deluge of water.

LESBIAN: In the Greek Isle of Lesbos the poetess Sappho wrote such passionate, lyrical verse that she and her female pupils were called Lesbians in the 6th Century BC.

LETTUCE: Supposed to have milk-like juice. L. *'lactus'* = milk.

LETHAL: In the Greek mythology the dead drank the water of the River Lethe to find oblivion and become lethargic.

LICK INTO SHAPE: Mothers of the animal kingdom generally treat their new born babies in this manner.

LIMOUSINE: A caped cloak worn in the province of *Limousin*, France - name given to enclosed motor car.

LOGANBERRY: Named after Judge Logan who bred it on his Californian orchard in the 19th Century.

LOOPHOLE: narrow opening in walls of medieval castles for defending archers to shoot at attackers with little fear to themselves. In later times this word came to mean a way out of trouble - especially with the law.

LUMBER: After the fall of the Roman Empire the Longobardis (Longbeards) from Central Europe settled in Northern Italy as bankers, pawnbrokers, etc. They spread to other parts of Europe including *Lombard* St in London where their premises included a *Lumber* store of unredeemed goods. In due course this word was taken to America by emigrants who cleared their land of unwanted trees - now called lumber.

MANURE: originally meant 'manual labour' based upon Latin. Later it came to include dung.

MARGARINE: from 'Margarita' = Latin for 'pearl', the colour of the extract of pigs' lard before dyes were added.

MARTINET: French army drill-master - a strict disciplinarian in the 17th Century.

MATIN(S): Morning Prayer from '*Matuta*', goddess of dawn - hence *matutinal*.

MAY-DAY!: distress call, from French '*M'aidez*!' = 'Help me!'

MAYFAIR: fashionable district in West London where *fairs* used to be held in May.

MAYONNAISE: a condiment created at Port *Mahon* in Minorca, Balearic Islands.

MEANDER: Verb from name of winding river in Asia Minor.

MONEY: from the goddess Juno *Moneta* in whose temple in the Roman Forum money was minted.

MOONRAKER: 18th Century Wiltshire rustics tried to rake the reflection of the moon from the village pond to gain this nickname which was adopted by the county regiment, 'Moonrakers'.

MOUNTEBANK: from It. *'montare-banco'* = to get up on a bench - to address and to persuade people to buy worthless goods.

NAVAL TERMS: Here follow naval terms used by the sea-faring nation of Britain:

BLAZER: a jacket sported by a skipper (i.e. a shipper) of *H.M.S. Blazer.*

BETTER OFF: in the nautical sense of well away from the shore WELL OFF: as in 'standing off', so that a ship avoids danger from reefs, shore batteries, etc. and to allow room to manoeuvre into a favourable position.

CLEAR THE DECKS: for action - or other modern activity.

GIVE ME A HAND (with the rigging): in rough weather a sailor had to hold the rail with one hand and to ask another to help with his free hand to do a task requiring two hands.

FIGUREHEAD: Originally a carving decorating the bow of a ship, now generally referring to a VIP heading an organisation without real responsibility.

KNOWING THE ROPES: experience teaches a mariner which ones to grasp.

LEFT HIGH AND DRY: when a ship runs aground on a sandbank or STRANDED: upon a beach (strand) the captain is as powerless as are people in a similar case.

MANAVELINS: surplus food taken from a ship's galley. Word used about 200 years ago, then broadened to mean kitchen waste. It was used by my mother and now me, but few others; yet I know no other word to describe vegetable peelings, tea bags, etc, consigned to the compost heap.

NAVE: roof of cathedral or large church, so called because it generally resembles an upturned ship.

NIPPERS: small pieces of rope - giving this nickname to small boys.

POSH: In the last century when wealthy people sailed by P and O to India (and back), they ordered luxury cabins on the port side to enjoy the cool north breeze and, for the same reason, the starboard side for the return trip. The booking clerk quoted '*Port Out*; *Starboard Home*' (or 'posh').

SKYSCRAPER: 18th century term for topmost sail of a ship.

'SAILING NEAR THE WIND': Steering ship as straight as possible while taking best advantage of the wind. The expression is now used pejoratively, as when a bishop once complained that some London theatres were 'sailing near the wind' by staging offensive material in the 1930s. This provoked a protest from Sir Alan Herbert (then 'A.P.H.' of Punch), a keen yachtsman, pointing out that to sail near the wind required great skill, worthy of applause. This led to the 'word war' of items sent in by Punch readers recording unwanted words and phrases invading our language at that time as they do, regrettably, now.

SON OF A GUN: one born on board in the shadow of guns.

STARBOARD: Early ships were steered with a paddle, as rudder, on the right side while the left was free for (un)loading in port.

STRIKE SAIL: to stop ship - likewise, in industry, *strikers* stop work and output.

TAKING WIND OUT OF SAILS: a ship suddenly slows owing to wind's change of direction or strength; so are we dismayed by sudden changes of mind or situation.

TARRED WITH THE SAME BRUSH: people who are equally objectionable.

PLAIN SAILING: from French '*plein*' = full - therefore, under *full sail*.

NICOTINE: *J. Nicot* introduced tobacco into France in the 16th Century.

Part V

NORMAL: from L. '*norma*' = carpenter's tool to check angles, measurements, etc.

NOSEY PARKER: Matthew Parker, Archbishop of Canterbury, in the mid 16th Century, gained a reputation for poking his rather long nose into other people's business.

'NUTS!': A contemptuous way to say 'no'. The one word reply to a German officer who advanced under a white flag to US General McAuley who held the vital cross roads at Bastogne against the final desperate advance of the German forces in the winter of 1944/45. Although surrounded, he held on until the enemy was forced back and he never surrendered. He was known henceforth as 'Nuts McAuley'.

OGRE: The Magyars or *Ugrians*, a cruel tribe of warriors, who were later known as *ogres*, invaded in the 10th Century and settled in what became *Hungary*.

OMELETTE: from Fr. '*lemele*' = knife-blade - used to lift omelette from pan?

OPPORTUNE: from Fr. - favourable wind bringing ships to *port*.

OSTRACISE: Gk. '*ostracon*' = potsherd. In ancient Greece an annual 'opinion poll' was held concerning any Athenian leader who was becoming too powerful or was suspected of treason. There were no voting papers, so the citizens scratched their votes upon the plentiful supply of broken pottery (*ostraka* - pl.). If the verdict went against the leader he was banished (*ostracised*) for a period of years or for life.

OUTRAM: the name of the mining engineer of the 19th Century who solved the problem of moving coal from the pithead by laying '*tram*' lines to a canal.

PALACE: after the Roman hill, *Palatium*, whereon Augustus Caesar built his house.

PAMPHLET: from 12th Century love poem - '*Pamphilus* seu de Amore'.

PANIC: The mischievous god '*Pan*' played his pipe to frighten and scatter

222

sheep.

PANTRY: originally a baker's store - from French *'pain'* = bread.

To PANDER: *Pandaros*, the character of evil designs in the works of Chaucer and Boccacio.

Stormy PETREL: sea-bird that treads on waves like *St Peter* in Matthew Ch. 4, v. 30.

PETTIFOGGING: describing the *Fugger* family of traders in medieval Augsburg where they were reputed to be *petty* and devious in their dealings.

PERIPATETIC: of the school of Aristotle and his habit of walking about while teaching. (c. 300 B.C.)

PERPLEX: from L. *'plexus'* = plait(ed), entangled, etc.

PERNICIOUS: unto death. L. *'nex'*.

PEP (talk): from *pepper*.

PHEASANT: The bird of the river *Phasis* in Asia Minor.

PHILANTHROPY: from the Gr. *'philos'* = love (of) *'anthropos'* = mankind.

PHILATELY: = Gk. *'ateleia'* = exemption from tax.

PINCHBECK: the name of 17th Century jeweller who used an alloy of copper and zinc to make cheap imitations of gold pieces.

POINT-BLANK: shot made by medieval archers aimed at small white (blank) centre of target.

PORCELAIN: from 'porcello' It. = little pig; the shape of the pure white cowrie shell.

PONDER: to consider or *weigh* mentally (L. 'pondus' = weight).

PRALINE: Sweet of sugared nuts created by the cook of the 17th Century Marshal Plessis - *Praslin*.

PRECOCIOUS: from *'coquere'* = to cook (L.) = fully cooked, experienced, mature (or 'hard-boiled'?).

PRETEXT: L. 'prae-*text*' (weave - textiles) = to make outward display.

PROTOCOL: based upon Gk. *'kolla'* = glue, to stick flyleaf into book for introduction.

QUARANTINE: Venice suffered so many plagues brought in by trading ships that they were made to wait 40 days (It. 'quaranta' = forty) in the lagoon for clearance.

RAMSHACKLE: from the 17th Century Icelandic word *'ramskakkr'* = very twisted, rickety, etc.

REBATE: now a small return of money; originally a falconer's recall of 'a bating hawk' which had soared away too soon.

RECALCITRANT: to kick out with heels L. *'calx'* = heel, or to behave similarly.

RECOIL: based upon L. *'culus'* (Fr. 'cul'; It. 'culo'), politely translated as 'the buttocks'. It is supposed that, when you withdraw suddenly from danger, you are likely to fall into a sitting posture.

RECONDITE: obscure; from L. *'condere'* = to hide.

REGATTA: the Venetian gondola race. It. *'rogatore'* = to compete.

REPTILE: from L. *'repere'* = to crawl.

RESILIENT: L. (re) *'salire'* = to jump (again).

RETAIL: Old Fr. *'retaille'* = piece cut off (It. *'tagliere'* = to cut).

REVEAL: to lift *veil*.

REVOKE: to call back.

RIVAL: one using the same stream L. *'rivus'*.

RODENT: L. *'rodere'* = to gnaw.

ROMANCE: medieval tale told in the *roman(ce)* tongue.

ROTHSCHILD: The 18th Century Jewish pawnbroker, Mayer Amschel, started business in the ghetto at Frankfurt. He prospered and rapidly developed it into a comprehensive bank; in due course his four sons opened branches in Naples, Paris, Vienna and London. The sign hanging outside the original pawnshop was a red shield - in German *'Rotschild'*.

RUMMAGE: from medieval French 'arrumager' - to load cargo, some of which was damaged on the voyage. This would be offered at special 'Rummage Sales' which now include any unwanted or outworn articles. Cynics refer to these as 'fêtes worse than death'.

SABOTAGE: Early this century there was a national rail strike in France when, in order to bring trains to a standstill, the strikers knocked out the wooden wedges called *'sabots'* (wooden shoes) which held the rails in position.

SALARY: Roman legionaries used to receive a ration of *salt 'salarium'* as part of their pay. Any soldiers who were unsatisfactory were described as *'not worth their salt'*.

SAMOVAR: Russian for 'self-boiler'.

SAMPHIRE: Herb of *Saint Pierre. Fr.* = St Peter.

SANDWICH: The 4th Earl of *Sandwich* ate meat in bread only, while gaming all day in the 18th Century.

SARCASM: Greek for *'tear flesh'*.

SARDONIC: from the Ancient Greek 'Sardo' = Sardinia where grew a poisonous herb, 'sardonia' - L. The islanders who ate it went into convulsions of sardonic laughter and many died with scornful grins on their faces.

SAVING FOR A RAINY DAY: In olden days farmers took their wives shopping when they went to the weekly market in their carts; but if the weather was fine at sowing or harvest time farmers were obliged to remain in the fields; so the wives saved their money for a rainy day.

to SHOOT ONE'S BOLT (arrow): refers to an archer who has used his last arrow.

SHELL: Last century, Marcus Samuel, a Jewish trader, specialised in *sea-shells* which he brought from the East for Victorians to decorate their homes. During his travels he stumbled upon the infant oil trade which received his increasing attention. His son, who became Lord Bearsted, built it up sensationally as the car industry expanded. For the brand name for his oil products he chose, you could be sure, - *Shell*.

SHERRY: fortified wine from *Jerez*, Spain, which the British pronounced 'sherry'. *Sack* (from French *'sec'*) is a dry version of it.

SHIBBOLETH: In the Bible (Judges 12.6) Hebrews used *Sibbolet* = ear of *corn*, as a pass-word to detect enemy spies who could not pronounce it correctly. It now indicates out-moded ideas. Perhaps *'corny'* is a by-product?

SHRAPNEL: air-burst gun ammunition timed to scatter pellets over enemy before touching the ground. Invented by General *Shrapnel* in the early 19th Century.

SIERRA: Jagged mountain peaks from the Spanish word for a saw.

SIESTA: Spanish for *'sixth hour'* - the time for repose.

SINCERE: In ancient Rome the metal workers made armour, weapons, pots and pans. Some of the less skilful finished their articles bearing scratches or cracks. Rather than discard them, they pressed wax into the blemishes to hide them. This annoyed the perfect craftsmen who proudly declared that their wares were *without (L. 'sine') wax (L. 'cerum')*, giving us the word *'sincere'*.

SINECURE: well-paid duty requiring little effort. L. *'sine'* = without, *'cura'* = care.

SKELETON: from Gk. *'skeletos'* = dried up.

SOLDIER: Roman Emperor Constantine minted the gold coin, *'solidus'*, to pay his *soldiers*.

STAMINA: from L. *'stamen'* = strong thread in warp of a loom.

STERLING: The early Normans minted coins stamped with a small *star* shape.

SUEDE: The French made special gloves called 'gants de *suède'* = gloves of Sweden.

SURE AS 'EGGS IS EGGS': not from farmyard, but mathematics: X = X - careless pronunciation in the 17th Century.

SYMPOSIUM: Greek for 'drinking party' - now meaning a (sober?) discussion group.

SHAMBLES: Butcher's slaughter-house - more generally the scene of carnage or muddle. A narrow medieval street in York is so named.

TABBY CAT: In old Baghdad a striped silk material was woven in the quarter named 'Attabiya'. The cloth found its way to England in the Middle Ages via France as 'tabis' and the English name 'tabby'. The striped brownish colours resembled those of the cat.

TACT: L. *'tactus'* = sense of touch.

TANK: armoured army vehicle given this code name for secrecy by W.

Part V

Churchill in World War 1.

TANTALIZE: from mythical King *Tantalus* of Phrygia who was tortured with thirst by being forced by captors to remain just out of reach of water.

TAUNT: from French '*tant pour tant*' = tit for tat, in the 16th Century - (so much for so much).

TAWDRY: from *St Audrey* (abbr. Etheldrida) of Ely whose lace was sold as cheap finery on St Audrey's Day in Ely market.

TEE-TOTAL: abstinence from alcoholic liquor. Temperance Society founded in Lancashire in 1833 by Robert Turner who stuttered in saying the word t-t-total.

TENNIS: Old Fr. '*tenez*' = take or receive; called by server.

THUG: member of criminal organisation in 18/19th Century India. Hindi = *thag*.
Marshall TITO: The nickname of the Jugoslav leader is best explained by an extract from the marvellous book 'Eastern Approaches' by Sir Fitzroy MacLean who joined him on behalf of the Allies during the war when the partisans were fighting the Germans: 'He would send for people and tell them what to do. 'You', he said, 'will do this; and you that', in Serbo-Croat: 'Ti to; ti to'.'

TRAGEDY: Greek theatres were originally built as settings for offering sacrifices to the gods. The victim was usually a goat = Gk. '*tragos*' - tragic for it!

TWEEZERS: from French '*étui*' = case for small instruments.

TYCOON: Japanese, '*Taikun*' = great prince.

VACILLATE: swaying from side to side etc. like the motion of a cow (L. '*vacca*'), especially from the rear.

VAMOOSE: Sp. '*vamos*' = let us go (away).

228

VAUDEVILLE: from *Vau de Vire*, Normandy, where 15th Century French poet, O. Basselin, was born; he composed convivial songs.

VENEZUELA: Early Spanish explorers found that the people of this country lived along networks of canals and so named it 'Venezuela' = little Venice.

VENDETTA: It. word from L. *'vindicta'* = vengeance.

VENISON: L. *'venari'* = to hunt (deer).

VERMICELLI, VERMIN: based upon L. *'vermis'* = worm.

VERMOUTH: from German *'wermut'* = wormwood, herb used in flavouring Vermouth wine.

VIABLE: able to live (Fr. *'vie'* = life).

VOLCANO: from *Vulcan*, Roman god of fire.

THE WEAK GO TO THE WALL: In medieval times there were no pews or seats in large churches and cathedrals where the congregation was expected to stand throughout the long services. However, a stone ledge was often built along the base of the walls so that the old or feeble could 'go to the wall' to rest.

WHIST: archaic = hush (*hist!*) silent.

DUMMY: archaic = *dumb* (silent). Words used in card games wherein few words are needed.

WHITTLE (away): Butcher's knife - to cut away.

WILDERNESS: *wild deer* area (ness).

WIN HANDS DOWN: from horse racing: when a jockey is nearing a very easy win he would let up on the reins.

WORSTED: 17th Century Huguenot weavers fled from persecution in the Low

Part V

Countries and some of the most skilful settled in *Worsted* near Norwich where the quality of their fine wool cloth became famous. See notes.

XEROS: from Gr. *'xeros'* = dry (printing process).

XYLOPHONE: from Greek *'xylon'* = wood, of which the instrument is made.

X-RAY: the code name given by the discoverer (Rontgen) before making further research into its use.

YANKEES: In New Amsterdam (later New York) Dutch settlers used the derisive nickname *'Jan Kees'* = cheese, for a stupid person.

ZEPHYR: from Gk. *Zephuros*, the god of the west wind.

ZODIAC: Gk. for sculptured animal-figure.

ZONE: Gk. for girdle.

NOTES: With reference to *'Bedlam'* and *'Worsted'* it is interesting to find these two words mentioned by Shakespeare:
'. . . proof and precedent of *Bedlam* beggars . . .'
(King Lear Act II Sc. 3)
'. . . a Knave, . . . a filthy worsted-stocking Knave'
(King Lear Act II Sc. 2)

Additional Derivations:

'BLESS YOU': In Ancient Rome a terrible plague smote the city. The symptom of those afflicted was an outburst of sneezing. The Pope learned that the victims were dying too fast for his priests to give a final blessing to them all. He therefore made a special edict so that anybody could give the blessing in his name to another who sneezed and would be likely to die. This custom still persists in all languages of Christendom.

CHORTLE: a blend of *chuckle and snort* . . . Lewis Carroll in 'Through the Looking Glass'.

CRESTFALLEN: from cockfighting when the loser's comb or crest collapses.

TOE THE LINE: which is marked along each side of the floor of the House of Commons two sword lengths apart to avoid bloodshed.

PEDIGREE: from the colouring or marks of a crane's foot suggesting descent. From the French '*pied de Grue*'.

APPENDIX I

'MIND YOUR LANGUAGE'

When I was at school 70 years ago my English teacher warned us against using inappropriate words, in forming sentences which created an amusing or curious meaning apart from that intended: e.g. 'When *a soldier had fired all his ammunition*, he could then fall back on his *bayonet*.' The following list suggests that these curiosities are still around:

Tea is the *bread and butter* of Asian countries (business talk).
The *property boom* has gone *through the roof* (financial comment).
The *shelling* left an *explosive* situation (war report).
After the week-long *transport strike*, Melbourne is *getting back on its feet*.
. . . only one Australian left in *the field* (Indoor Tennis Tournament).
It was a *day*long *nightmare*.
Melbourne ought to host the *Olympic* Games because of its better *track record*.
We know she can *medal* (not 'interfere' as it seemed, but *win an event*).
The *gun amnesty* has *triggered* off the right result (surrender of illegal weapons).
Mr Bush's *refusal* to *ban automatic guns triggered* off some criticism in USA.
Lendl (2 sets down) had an *ace* up his sleeve to *checkmate* his opponent.
The C. Government *snuffed out* the people's *thirst* for Democracy.
He *regrouped* his game (Tennis *singles*).
The Government will *put a floor* under the *Housing Industry*.
The South *Electricity* Corporation *remains in the dark* about policies.
Queensland has a new Premier as the result of a *ground swell* of opinion from the Party's *grassroots*.
An American trader succeeded in importing solid *ice* to California where it sells like *hot cakes*.
We are looking at a *mid-air collision straight down the barrel* (Airport Control after near-miss).
People should be put *ahead of cars* (to be run over?).
Government should not treat *liquor tax* as a *milking cow*.
Mr. Gerry Malone, a Tory *retread* who lost Aberdeen South in 1987, but secured Winchester in 1992 (UK Election).
We are *exploring every avenue* we can *get our teeth into* (Government spokesman).

233

Appendix I

Goliath casts the *first stone* in take-over battle.
This group plays a variety of *wind* instruments with *tongue in cheek.*
The *oarsman* hopes to win the *rowing* event *on home soil.*
If English was good enough for Jesus, it's good enough for me!
Farmers are getting their *high-flying* policy *off the ground.*
The future of the country *aerodrome* is *up in the air.*
The security of the (English) *Channel* tunnel is being assessed *in great depth.*
The *Great White Shark* is now *in full flight* (Golf Commentary).
'The children's wing has a brand-new *spanking* nursery.' (Health official).
After a much-loved vicar died in an English village, his obituary in the subsequent parish magazine ran: - he was *literally* the *father of every child* in the village.
If we pursue that course, we shall *literally* be caught with our *pants down* (Government debate).
The carport at Phillip Island was *literally* a *sea of bikes.*
The jockey *literally* carried his horse past the winning post.
In the final round 'Ian Baker-Finch *literally throttled his opponents*' (TV Golf Report).
Lendl *literally* cut the young German to pieces. ('What bloody man is that?' Macbeth, Act I.)
The loser was *literally steamrolled* (flat on his face?)
They *show-cased* their skills (Arts, etc. display).
Louis XIV's orchestra played *chamber music* to put him to bed.
She is the First Lady of *conspiratology* (writer of 'Whodunits').
Mrs Thatcher was *bitten* by the man she *treated as a mat.*
It will take a little time for his *lawn mowing business to get off the ground.*
Mr Major should appoint new ministers to replace those now past the '*sell-by date*' (comment from UK).
Doctor hits out at boxing.
Brawler-van (for police to pick up late-night drunks).
He was *banging an issue on the table* (from politics).
An *anti-arthritic joint* walk (a charity effort).
The *liquidation* of the *swimming pool* (removal because unprofitable).
The *cook-off* starts tomorrow (competition for chefs).

The following items are culled from the quarterly journals of the Queen's English Society of which I am a member:

'Don't kill your wife with work - let electricity do it.'
'Woman wants cleaning three days a week.'
The marriage was *consummated* by the Archbishop of Canterbury (Royal Wedding on BBC TV).
Shell stated that *oil price increases* were already *in the pipe-line.*
Rate of pay *consummate* with experience (notice in Job Centre).
... Henry VIII had six wives and he died of *consummation* (schoolboy's essay).
... 'to *humiditise*' (spray water in greenhouse).
'disinstitutionisation'
... no-one can *crystal-ball* the future . . .
'Presidentialisation'
'theatric'
'releasability'
'Singaporeanised'
'virtuousic'
'skulduggerism'
'globalisation'
'conspicuity'
'retrenchees'
'gesturapaedic programme'
... 'amputees' (people who have lost limbs)
'prioritisation'
'incentivation'
... 'competition open to all ages and *calibres*'
'humanitarianise' (make human)
'When did you become *radicalised*?' (Politician interviewed)
'scapegoatism'
'nakediffity' (nude)
'dezincification' (removing zinc)
Wheat-growers have not reached the land of *milk and honey.*
A broad-gauge international perspective (US News)
Bike-a-thon (bicycle road race)
'telethon' (charity session for 'phoned offers)
'choc-aholic'
'village-isation'
'trampathon' : 'sailathon' : 'tidierthon' (whole community clearing rubbish)
'dogathon' (dog show)

Appendix I

'Samaritanathon'
'Aboriginalisation' (of the Government Department)
'Feelings of *Antagony*' (and Cleopatra?)
'*acoustician*' (who tests suitability of concert halls)
Presidentiable - possible next US President appealathon.
The Vicar will be at the General Synod in London next week. Please pray for the Synod at this time (English Parish Magazine)
Addenda: These *avenues* must be *addressed*.
The *liquidation* of the *swimming pool* to save costs.
It depends upon our *indivuation*
The Albanians *sardined* themselves into a ship for Italy
We have weeded out all the bad eggs.
For some time Gorbachev has been *walking* on a tight rope on the edge of a *precipice*.
A Government official, apologising for a computer error causing private information to go to wrong people, urged them to have a good '*forgettery*'.
You have *cooked* your *goose*; now you must *lie* in it.
Royal expenditure has reached *gastronomical* proportions.
The Automobile Association should adopt a *middle-of-the-road* policy.
She was a lady of easy *vice*.
I shall *mould* the boys like *clay* in the hunter's *snare*.
You must not hanker after the *fish pots* of Egypt.
Do not make a *mountain* out of a *tea-cup*.
Negotiations are being kept at a *low-key profile*.
A *verbal* agreement is not worth the *paper* its *written* on.
I don't know how you can cook in such a *circumcised* space.
Teachers had *aperients* before luncheon.
There will be a *wild elephant* stall at the Fête.
Fifty miles as the *cock crows*.
The choir should have *pitch forks* to keep the note.
The school orchestra played Beethoven: Beethoven *lost*.
He *electricuted* his audience.

APPENDIX II

MEMORIES OF WORKSOP IN WORLD WAR I

In the last century Canon Woodard preferred to locate schools of his foundation on isolated hill-tops away from the perils of civilisation. For example, we saw no girls, except a few maid-servants, from the beginning to end of term. Apart from the Headmaster and his wife, who had no children, I cannot recall any married members of the staff during my period from 1915 to 1921. However, a couple of romances burgeoned among them because the English master married the Art mistress and the History master married the matron; but it was noticed that they were not welcomed back after their weddings; it seemed that, having committed matrimony, they were banished from the Garden of Eden. In any case there were no married quarters in those days.

As decades passed many developments and improvements have taken place; the school buildings have doubled; rugger posts have replaced soccer goals; hockey was yet to make its début. The archaeological remains of our swimming pool lurk, brooding on the chilly past, in the shadow of the magnificent structure of today. In my time the Chapel organ was powered by the muscle of youths who wished to be included in the annual choir outing or were doing penance for misdemeanours. Their efforts were adequate for normal music; but during fortissimo passages, despite frantic pumping, the bellows were prone to change key into a hollow groan.

I heard that the boys are now able to wash in warm water and to eat bacon, eggs, etc. for breakfast in addition to traditional porridge, bread and margarine; indeed, at a recent reunion, I read a week's menus on the notice board which rivalled those of a star hotel.

However, we survived and my era has produced at least one octogenarian whose name modesty forbids me to mention. I was escorted to school from Harrogate by Keith Morrison who later left school to join the Royal Navy before the end of that war. In the last war he was second-in-command to Captain E.S.F. Fegan, of Scandinavian descent, on the armed liner Jervis Bay. Both lost their lives on escort duty when their ship engaged the enemy at hopeless odds to enable their convoy to scatter to safety.

I arrived at Worksop shortly after the outbreak of World War I at the same time as the late lamented and my life-long friend, Leslie Taylor, whose devoted service to the school will surely never be forgotten. It was also the first year of the rule of the Rev. Marchant Pearson as Headmaster who coped very well with the wartime difficulties and with him you always felt in the presence of a gentleman. I have never forgotten his yardstick for good behaviour revealed to us when some boys were arraigned before us for unsavoury talk. He said: 'When you are in doubt about voicing your thoughts, ask yourself this question: would I mind my mother overhearing me?' On another occasion, during a sermon for the benefit of school-leavers, he spoke these immortal words: 'Always remember that it is not what you do that matters but what you are.' Mr Pearson took us for Scripture lessons and used them as a vehicle for ramming home certain aspects of English grammar. He was fanatically keen (and rightly so) upon pronunciation and punctuation. We were taught to say eeeleven instead of 'leven or eleven, and I still say eeeleven to the present day. Also to bite on our consonants. Full stops had to terminate every abbreviation and sentence. On the blackboard huge slashes of chalk represented commas and for full stops he described circles as wide as 10p. pieces and filled them in with chalk. By the end of the period the sacred writings were so interlaced with crotchets and quavers that the result looked like a page from an Oratorio.

The second Master was Mr G.A. O'Meara, a Cambridge Wrangler whose wizardry in Mathematics filled us with awe. In class he bumbled along, soon covering the blackboard with a mass of signs, letters and figures while we sat bemused and bewildered – except for a bespectacled youth in the front row. Occasionally, by way of diversion, Mr O'Meara would stop in midsum and chalk in bold capitals the legend: 100 LINES, covering this with his hand, he would invite the boy who was dozing to state what was underneath. The culprit would make a wild, vain guess; the hand was raised – and he got the message. Mr O'Meara suffered the endearing in ability to pronounce words containing the letter 'L' for which he substituted 'V'. Perversely, he seemed to choose such words as frequently as possible. For example, when I went to say goodbye at the end of my last term he said: 'Ah Norrington, I hear that you are going to Vive near Vondon; that will be rather jovvy won't it?' When the time came for him to retire from the housemastership of Cross (now know as Mason) his boys clubbed together to buy him a set of pipes. The presentation was made on his last night after a short graceful speech by the Head of House. Deeply moved, the good man paused for a moment to control his emotion and then he declared 'I'm fvabbergasted'. The rest of his speech was drowned by affectionate cheers. Mr O'Meara's version of this word was adopted in my family life: instead of being astonished or appalled by anything, 'fvabbergasted' seemed more expressive.

During this time the academic life of Worksop was dominated by the study of French. Qualified linguists of British and French nationality had been called away to war service; but from the neutral zone there descended upon us a formidable Dutchman named 'ten Haaf' whom we called 'Quarter-Break' because we used to enjoy (until he came) fifteen minutes free time at 10.30 each morning. His dedication to an alien tongue was astonishing. He set about his task with tremendous gusto, sparing neither us nor himself. Like many Martinets he was kind out of school; but his idea of our ability to digest his vast quantity of 'Prep' was, to say the least, optimistic. On waking each morning we no longer hailed our fellows with such words as 'good morning'; 'How are you?' or 'What shall we do today?' The standard greeting was: 'Done your French?' Even this was a rhetorical question, for the answer was always a gloomy 'No'. Our pockets were stuffed with French books to be withdrawn and studied surreptitiously at every possible opportunity – in bed and bath; in Hall and Chapel; in places unmentionable. Every morning we had a free hour after breakfast which had to be spent out of doors in the open air. There we strolled in twos and threes, muttering over our French Grammars like Tibetan monks over their prayer wheels. The day was conveniently divided into three parts. In the morning you swotted feverishly the oral French left over from the night before; in the afternoon you did the imposition arising from your shortcomings in the morning class; at evening 'prep' periods forsaking all other, you did written French. Other masters protested that they were not receiving a fair share of our labours. All in vain. They were thankful for a captive audience in their own periods – that is, if they remembered to confiscate our French books at the start of their lessons.

Later, a deceptively frail young lady arrived to teach us Latin.

We looked forward to some relaxing hours wherein we could do more French revision. This illusion was soon rudely shattered, for we now had among us a feminine bundle of dynamite. Even Mr ten Haaf reeled under the impact. Miss Stonehouse brought the dead language to life by blending some interesting history of Ancient Rome with her instruction; but she also gaily piled on loads of work far beyond our scope. We were fvabbergasted, but too chivalrous to complain. The battle of the languages raged for several terms. Then, with Miss Stonehouse winning and ourselves cracking under the strain, rescue came from an unexpected quarter. The prefect, Eric Williamson, having wooed her discreetly, led her away from us and to the altar soon after he left school, and they lived happily ever after.

A scourge afflicting half the school was physical – chilblains. Every winter our fingers took on the appearance of bunches of bananas, red and raw, severely impairing our work and play. We had come to accept our fate with patient resignation when an Irish nursing sister of fearsome mien and fiery temperament joined the staff. She came; she saw; she made up her mind to conquer – and she did! Vast quantities of cod liver and malt were imported in containers the size of oil drums. We lined up in front of one of these each morning, while Sister plunged a spoon into the sticky mass and wound a dose onto it with a couple of brisk up and down motions of her wrist. Then, with a rapid thrust, she aimed it at the next mouth. Woe betide the boy who was not ready, for he received a sharp clout on the cheek with the loaded spoon and tottered off to lick himself clean as best he could. After Malt Parade we were ordered to run three times round the school buildings and to report back to Sister who felt our hands for warmth; but we all trotted off to sit on the hot water pipes, heating each hand alternately while the other clutched the inevitable French book. Exceptions were two young gentlemen with religious leanings who slipped dutifully into orbit, cheered on as they flitted past by the perambulating devotees of French.

A feature of Worksop before the invention of Common Entrance was the 'Prep' Dormitory, where Matron was 'in loco parentis' to the very young. She never failed to visit each of us every night to enquire anxiously: 'Have you been to Court today?' After initial puzzlement we adopted the right spirit and gave the appropriate answer. But I have never heard this elegant term since; and I have often wondered how it originated; perhaps it was a relic from the Age of chivalry. One of the Prep. Dorm, inmates, named Norton, used to entertain us almost nightly with tales from the Magnet Library. A public spirited lad, he used his holidays to accumulate a liberal fund of material which he related vividly and illegally after 'lights out'. Sometimes Miss Arnison crept into the entrance, hidden from the narrator's view, and stood listening attentively. She was never in a hurry to interrupt and I suspect that she, too, enjoyed the stories.

Life at Worksop was not insupportably harsh; it was more mellow at the end of my time than at the beginning, and now the arrival of girls will have had a further civilising influence.

In those early days Public Schools were traditionally a mixture of monastery and penitentiary. If new boys were filled with trepidation on arrival, it must be remembered that most of them were about eight years old. The raw material had not been moulded into shape by Mr Sowerbutts, a splendid teacher, and later at Ranby.

Our prestige and popularity rested mainly upon prowess at sport, and I suppose that this remains so. Regrettably, however, our attitude towards learning was reactionary. A state of cold war existed between Master and pupil when it came to Academics and you were considered a black leg if you studied too hard. We used to go slow and work to rule as a matter of routine – with the exception, of course, of French and Latin.

I am persuaded that present day scholars are more enlightened; perhaps they are aware of the sacrifices made by their parents to pay their fees; anyhow, I like to think so.

If, in conclusion, I am entitled to send a message to Worksopians of today and tomorrow, it is this:

Spurn not the Banquet spread before you! Five years are little time to taste every dish; indulge, nay, gorge yourselves while you may.

C. A. Norrington
1915–1921

Nefertiti   4.99
Before Wallis   7.99
Harriet   4.99
Ava   9.99
M.S.   5.99
                  ————
                  33.99
                   3.00
                  ————
                  36.99